Men Together

Portraits of Love, Commitment, and Life

Essays by ANDERSON JONES • Photographs by DAVID FIELDS

RUNNING PRESS
PHILADELPHIA · LONDON

Text © 1997 by Anderson Jones
Photographs © 1997 by David Fields

Printed in China

9   8   7   6   5   4   3   2   1
Digit on the right indicates the number of this printing

Library of Congress Cataloging-in-Publication Number 96-69231

ISBN 0-7624-0062-5

This book may be ordered by mail from the publisher. Please include $2.50 for postage and handling.
But try your bookstore first!

Running Press Book Publishers
125 South Twenty-second Street
Philadelphia, Pennsylvania 19103-4399

For those who have died in the name of love, for those who love

whomever they wish, and for my mother whom I will love forever.

And for Mrs. Guillen who told me in the seventh grade

that I would write a book someday—and I didn't believe her.

—AJ

For my mom and dad, who've always encouraged me to pursue

a career that I love, and who have taught me how to enjoy a complicated life.

—DF

Contents

PREFACE

This is a book about ordinary men—some of whom are living extraordinary lives—experiencing the ordinary miracle of an enduring, loving relationship with another man.

When David and I began working on this book nearly two years ago, we worried that every couple would tell the same story: *We met, we fell in love, we lived happily ever after, the end*. Instead, each of the twenty-nine stories that make up *Men Together* is a multifaceted and wonderfully individual testament to love, life, and joint perseverance in the face of any number of obstacles—family disapproval, social ostracism, sickness, death and survival, financial strife, and heartbreak among them.

The men in this book are indeed brave souls who have opened up some of the most intimate parts of their lives to us. They share their stories here because they believe in the power of commitment and because they know that our society's penchant for intolerance and ignorance tends to keep stories like theirs out of sight, hidden from other men who hunger for role models, who would find hope in knowing that it is possible to love another person in a happy, healthy, lasting gay relationship.

But this volume, by its nature, is incomplete. Many of the men featured here have achieved an uncommon degree of independence from the strictures of the corporate environment, the discriminatory practices of the local school board, the suffocating rules of the moral majority. As successful artists, business owners, pop-culture icons, writers, politicians, doctors, and designers, they all, of course, have undertaken considerable risk by acknowledging—and celebrating—their love in this book. But they are not the only examples of long-term couples among us.

Gay men—and gay couples—are indeed everywhere, but missing from these pages are the members of tiny rural communities, the junior employees building their careers in potentially hostile work environments, the public-school teachers who fear the loss of their jobs, and the thousands of other men who are living less celebrated, more anonymous lives in small towns and big cities everywhere. They must continue to find their own, quieter ways of teaching those around them about sacrifice, compromise, and devotion against the odds.

We are disappointed that we can't present here more of the colors of the rainbow flag. It's not because we didn't try. Although we found a few interracial couples and one African-American couple who agreed to share their stories with us, most of the men of color we approached felt uncomfortable appearing in a book like this one, when coming out might threaten their income or ties to their families. Our long walk home is not over.

Still, we are pleased by what we've been able to accomplish. We hoped to create a book a son could present with pride to his parents, to help them understand a part of his life they may not know. We hoped young gay people would be able to flip through these pages and see themselves—as they are now or as they hope to be ten years from now.

We wanted to send gay men of all ages a message that, just like their straight friends and peers, they too can experience a loving relationship that will last a lifetime or more. We tried to make this book a reminder that love does not require anybody's stamp of legitimacy in order to exist, that it is blind to gender, race, and age, and that through hard work and commitment it will continue to thrive no matter what the world says.

We hope *Men Together* will remind you that the struggles, setbacks, frustrations, and triumphs you've experienced in your own relationships are not yours alone.

ACKNOWLEDGMENTS

This book would have been impossible without: my dear friend and editor Brian Perrin (who always knew I could do this),

my transcribers Beverly and Jerry, Sjohnna (who will write more books than I), Tracy (who will read them all),

Chad (who knows everything), Paul (who always calls), and Dr. Bugeja (who helped me find the way).

And a special thanks to my friends and associates at Turner.

—AJ

I owe great thanks to the subjects of this book for being so enthusiastic during the photography sessions;

and to Ken Newbaker for his thoughtful design and photo-editing, and for understanding that

sometimes in trying to create a pearl one might have to tolerate a little irritation.

—DF

DESMOND CHILD AND CURTIS SHAW

Hₑ's known in music circles for writing the songs that get stuck in your head.

If you know any song by Bon Jovi, he probably wrote it—he's responsible for "You Give Love a Bad Name," "Livin' On a Prayer," and "Bad Medicine," among others. He convinced Aerosmith's Steven Tyler that "Dude Looks Like a Lady" would be good for his band's career; he also wrote their biggest recent hits, "Angel" and "Crazy." He put the words "How Can We Be Lovers (If We Can't Be Friends)" into Michael Bolton's mouth and gave Cher the ballad "We All Sleep Alone."

But unless you're an avid reader of liner notes—or a fan of obscure early 1990s music trivia (he once tried a solo career of his own)—you've probably never heard of Desmond Child.

And that's precisely how Curtis Shaw, Desmond's partner of eight years, likes it. "It's a relief that I don't have to go through what Steve Tyler does," says Curtis. "We have the best of both worlds—we're in that world but we have anonymity."

They also have the spoils of a successful career in rock & roll. Their double-walled Miami Beach home—they call it "Four Palms"—sits on the Intracoastal Waterway just fifteen minutes from South Beach. It's a Spanish-style hacienda with a red-tiled roof and an open, greenery-filled courtyard perfect for entertaining. Platinum and gold albums wallpaper the office that Desmond and Curtis share. They've sold their house in Santa Monica, California, and they're building a rustic-looking A-frame in Nashville, Tennessee, so that Curtis can expand his country-music writing career. Four Palms is filled with artifacts from their travels—exotic lamps, antique weapons, a window pane from Morocco, and artwork from all over Europe.

It doesn't seem like a life that would be hard to get used to, but Curtis says it was difficult at first. When he began living with Desmond, Curtis was working as a waiter in New York City. Desmond was already making millions as a songwriter-producer. The disparities in their lifestyles were enormous.

DESMOND CHILD (LEFT) AND CURTIS SHAW IN THE POOL AT FOUR PALMS.

"I kept saying '*Your* house, *your* this, *your* that,' because I felt like in some ways I wasn't contributing monetarily for this," Curtis says. "But as things have gone on, Desmond is the first to say '*Our* house, *our* life.' I work my ass off running our lives. So, I have no problem now saying this is our life, this is our house."

"I see a partnership," Desmond says. "He does his part, and I do my part."

Initially, it may have seemed a little more like a business partnership than a romantic one. Desmond had tasted success but continued to live in a Virginia commune where he'd lived for years. He didn't want to take care of himself, he admits, and was desperate for a mate because, as he says, "I'm high maintenance."

Desmond encouraged Curtis to come live with him in California, where he could pursue his acting career—and take care of Desmond.

"I really couldn't be alone anymore," Desmond says. "It was sort of like we were two people that needed each other and we clicked. I had already been with a couple of nuts and I felt like I needed to be with a person who was emotionally stable, someone who wasn't going to jerk me around emotionally."

Curtis's friends thought it was a bad idea. It would be unlike him—usually so conservative and careful—to pack up and move west to be with a man he barely knew.

"Part of me loved that," Curtis says. "I just felt my intuition said 'Do it, go for it. Life is about risk.' So, I took a risk."

About two years after the couple moved in together, Desmond got a recording deal with Elektra and began touring to promote his album. Gradually his career began to crowd his relationship with Curtis.

At the same time, Curtis felt like he was losing himself. "I became the person I thought he wanted me to be," he says. "I was

his lackey. His personality, his ego totally changed."

"Oh, did not," Desmond interjects.

"No, it happened," Curtis continues. "You got a little high on yourself. And, actually, the best thing that could have happened for us was that his album didn't take off. If it was a major success, we probably would not be together now. You were a pain."

"I was not," Desmond protests good naturedly. "You're just exaggerating."

"I felt that he wasn't really involved in our relationship," Curtis says. "I'm very sensitive and I sensed he wasn't there for our relationship."

"It's true," Desmond sighs. "I was just on my locomotive going forward. But I finally realized what was important to me. And I recommitted myself, and things have been great ever since. I love Curtis and I respect him."

Indeed, once Desmond's solo career ended and the couple moved to Florida to escape the riots, fires, and earthquakes of life in Los Angeles, things brightened considerably. And as they rediscovered one another they began to think about expanding their family to include children. Especially Desmond, who sees two gay men building a family as a defiant move, but a necessary one.

"I just read in the *New York Times* where some senator said that gay people shouldn't be allowed to get married because they don't stay together," Desmond says bitterly, "and because they can't have families. But we *can* have families.

"Those things make you angry at your country. And there's an isolation that you're made to feel. So if you notice, there are two walls between me and the outside world here. I want to create my own world where there's none of that feeling of second-class citizenship. So we're looking into options and we *will* have our family."

"*Some senator said that gay people shouldn't be allowed to get married because they don't stay together and because they can't have families. But we can have families. Those things make you angry at your country. And there's an isolation that you're made to feel.*"

CHARLES POWELL AND STEVEN ZORN

When Steven Zorn left Philadelphia and began living with Charles Powell in Virginia Beach, Virginia, four years ago, he actually moved in with two people.

"I'm bipolar," Charles explains, grabbing Steven's hand for a moment as they sit together on their comfy living room couch.

"You see," he continues, "there are two of me. There's the totally depressed one on this end and the totally elated one on this end. It's a circle. And my life is nothing more than passing from one phase to the other."

It's an open secret among Charles and Steven's closest friends, but not one that Charles talks about often. He says everything in his life is now structured around the fact that he's manic-depressive. He owns his own business because he believes he is unemployable. He no longer carries credit cards, to avoid the temptation of a sudden splurge.

"When you're manic, the world is yours, and you can buy, buy, buy, buy, buy, buy, buy . . . clothes, cars, houses, people—anything.

You just buy because the world belongs to you," says Charles. "Then all of a sudden you start coming down and the credit card bills start coming in, and the bounced checks and reality come into focus. Then you're in depression."

The forty-nine-year-old interior designer used to manage his illness with medication that only made him feel worse. Now he gardens instead. The tiny white clapboard house he shares with Steven—just blocks from Virginia's coast—has one of the most well-tended flower beds in the neighborhood.

Charles stopped taking therapeutic drugs when his last relationship ended.

"I went cold turkey on reality," he says.

And it changed his life. Just in time—because in the midst of working through paying off his debts, regaining control of his unpredictable moods, trying to maintain a certain level of calmness and a firm grip on reality, he met Steven.

"If I hadn't been into that, I never would have wanted Steven

CHARLES POWELL (LEFT) AND STEVEN ZORN NEAR THEIR VIRGINIA BEACH HOME.

"*I*t *sounds really awful,*
but when he's on a downslide
I get some peace and quiet—
we have our own lives,
we do our own things. When
he's up, we do things together.
When he's not, what he really
wants is his own space.
I understand that. It really
has to be worked through."

around at all because he wasn't exciting," Charles admits. "He's wonderfully steady, and I found that Steven contributed to the calmness."

Steven's been learning to live with both sides of Charles and says it's not as difficult as it may seem.

"You cannot live with someone who's bipolar and not be excited," Steven says, adjusting the wildly colored frames of his glasses. "It sounds really awful, but when he's on a downslide I get some peace and quiet—we have our own lives, we do our own things. When he's up, we do things together. When he's not, what he really wants is his own space. I understand that. It really has to be worked through."

"I'll say to Steven," Charles begins, " 'In your wildest imagination, did you ever think you would wind up with a bipolar interior designer who is fifteen years older than you are?' And he'll say, 'Never.' "

"But," says Steven, "here we are."

When Charles and Steven met, introduced by a mutual friend in a local bar, Charles characteristically played hard to get. Instead of giving Steven his phone number he revealed only the name of his design studio, which meant that Steven had to track him down.

"I didn't pay any attention to you at all," Charles says. "I was perfectly happy by myself and I certainly didn't want someone who was obviously much younger than I."

It may have taken the rest of that summer, but eventually the two began dating, and Steven sold his house in Philadelphia.

"I moved here so suddenly," Steven says, "it wasn't even a conscious thing." Indeed, it was so sudden that even Charles didn't realize what had happened. Friends had to sort of tell him.

"How long has he lived here?" they would ask.

"He doesn't live here. He has his own place," Charles would say.

"Does he sleep here?"

"Yeah."

"Are his clothes here?"

"Yeah."

"Does he ever go to his other place?"

"No."

"It sounds like he lives here."

"And I had to admit," Charles says, his hand on his forehead, reliving the surprise all over again, "that he does live here."

Adds Steven, "It was just so natural—so evolutionary rather than revolutionary."

Four years ago the couple planned to move away from Virginia Beach—probably closer to Washington, D.C., where Steven often works as a writer and producer for the Discovery Channel. Charles's business wasn't doing as well then as it is now, and a move made sense. Today, not so much. They've found a house built in 1925 that sits even closer to the ocean than their current home, and they're getting ready to move.

"We bought it together," Charles explains. "And it's the closest thing we can have to a marriage because we entered into a partnership agreement."

"So the quality of our life is wonderful as a married couple," Steven says. "The quality of life is good here. It's safe. It's clean."

It's also serene—a home where together, just the two of them, they can enjoy the cool calmness of reality.

WILLIAM DUFTY AND DENNIS FAIRCHILD

The evidence of William Dufty's celebrity life can be found throughout the cozy, well-preserved home he's shared with Dennis Fairchild for the past ten years: A self-portrait sketch of John Lennon reading Bill's best-selling self-help diet guide, *You Are All Sanpaku*, with Lennon's signature scribbled along the bottom, dated Nov. 7, 1968. A framed Billie Holiday stamp in the kitchen—a remembrance of one of Bill's best friends and the godmother to his son, whose autobiography, *Lady Sings the Blues*, Bill co-wrote. A snapshot of Bill taken by his late wife, film diva Gloria Swanson.

The photo was taken in 1966, when Bill and Gloria lived in Hawaii. The faded image still clearly shows why Dennis—or anyone for that matter—would fall in love with Bill: he is movie-star handsome. Now eightysomething, Bill is still ruggedly good looking, his hair heartily seasoned with salt and pepper. He still wears a custom-made Cartier dog tag around his neck—a gift Swanson had made for him. It bears Bill's name and social security number, along with the inscription: "Under my hat."

"That was Gloria's joke," Bill explains smiling, "because I was a wandering man."

Bill and Dennis met through Dennis's acupuncturist in 1982. Dennis wasn't interested at first but he soon became an integral part of Bill's life as the caretaker for Bill's ninety-five-year-old mother.

"I loved coming and being with his mom and cooking for her," Dennis says. "She was wonderful."

He also looked after Bill, helping out with the cooking whenever Bill visited from New York. They became very close. When Swanson died in 1983 it was Dennis who let Bill know.

"Every death has a birth," Dennis says. "That was the birth of our relationship."

Although he admits having been attracted to Dennis—"I thought he was very cute . . ."—Bill doesn't necessarily consider himself a gay man. "I'm primarily very heterosexual, but I got

WILLIAM DUFTY (LEFT) AND DENNIS FAIRCHILD AT THEIR HOME OUTSIDE DETROIT.

19

"*W*e're just one of those odd commodities that happens to be a color of the rainbow."

curious," he explains.

Bill believed he would die within ten years of his wife and felt he needed someone to take care of him, but he says, quoting Billie Holiday, "I'm not into exclusivité about anything."

As his and Dennis's relationship blossomed, Bill slowly began to appreciate Dennis's gifts as a working astrologer and psychic.

"Gloria was big into astrology," Bill says. "She would not make a move without consulting an astrologer in Beverly Hills. She wouldn't consider buying a house or signing a book contract. Dennis became a part of my life. I never imagined myself staying in Michigan."

After Bill's mother died, he and Dennis moved into her house full-time. Their initial plan was to renovate it and sell it, but once the project was finished, they decided to make the house their own. They bought it together and became the first same-sex couple to own a house jointly in Birmingham, Michigan, with both their names on the deed.

The most striking difference between the two men is their age. Dennis is thirty-five years younger than Bill. Dennis says this never crossed his mind.

"I never from the first day thought anything other than, 'This is the coolest person in the world I've ever met,' " he says.

But it did cross Bill's mind. "I thought he was after my money," he jokes over dinner in their living room. "I didn't want to be arrested as a child molester." The smile on his face straightens under his bushy mustache as he says, "I could not imagine my grandfather, as I remember my grandfather, having an affair with some guy in a small town after my grandmother died, you know? But now I can appreciate it—why not?"

"We're just one of those odd commodities that happens to be a color of the rainbow that is not included in a box of Crayola crayons," Dennis says, dismissing the thought with his animated hands. "But it's a good color."

Bill sees Dennis filling the role of caretaker, not that Bill needs much caretaking—he mows the front yard, walks about five miles a day, and hurries off in the snow to the neighborhood store to track down some orange juice when Dennis realizes they have none.

Dennis sees Bill not only as his lover but as a mentor, coach, best friend, and favorite editor—Bill edits the books Dennis writes on astrology, palm reading, the Tarot, and Feng Shui. Theirs is an intellectual relationship, Dennis explains, that became a romantic one.

"He taught me things that I didn't know," Dennis says. "I could tell him what was cool—what was going on that maybe he didn't have his finger on. Ours was just major bonding. I would like to grow up and be like him. It was never initially a sexual thing."

"Obviously—no one would ever think of me that way, which is fine," Bill says dryly.

"Oh no," Dennis says with a knowing smile. "You're cute. He's got a good butt."

JAMES L. CORAN AND WALTER A. NELSON-REES

*J*ames Coran and Walter Nelson-Rees are the grandparents that every gay man wishes he had.

To begin with, their apartment is *perfect* for visiting. It's a fabulous two-bedroom high-rise that's painted in twenty-seven different shades, has wrap-around floor-to-ceiling windows, and is located in the heart of San Francisco's Russian Hill.

More importantly, they've spent thirty-eight years of their lives together and are still in love. They have a strong sense of history and are full of the wisdom that comes with experience. Together, they've watched this thing called the gay movement evolve from its quiet infancy to its very vocal adulthood.

"The whole gay rights matter today is a very vital one," says Walter. "We admire people who have a cause but we are not really participants in the gay-bar scene or the gay-bathhouse scene. We are not activists. We have never been persecuted. But we have very strong feelings about the fact that as gay people, we do have to watch our steps."

Walter watched his step for twenty-one years as a research professor at the University of California at Berkeley before he retired in 1981 to start an art-dealing business with Jim. He says academia was "a very strict environment."

"There was no way he could have been out," says Jim. "Even when he became director of the lab and worked with the National Institutes of Health, I don't think anyone knew. Not a word was said."

"It's not discussed," Walter adds, "I would have the staff over for charades. These were all straight people. Jim would leave the house. It was simply a matter of being able to avoid answering questions."

But today Jim and Walter are always answering questions about their relationship. Inadvertently they have become role models to their younger gay friends.

"We don't understand what kind of role models we are," Walter says. "The thing that amazes us is that a number of our young

JAMES CORAN (RIGHT) AND WALTER NELSON-REES ON THE MARIN HEADLANDS OVERLOOKING THE GOLDEN GATE BRIDGE.

friends are so concerned about having a relationship. And this is fine, but it's something that's brand new to us. We started living together simply because we wanted to live together."

"There was no map," says Jim.

They have even become role models to their straight friends. Over the years they've had long conversations with a Navy officer and his wife about what it means to be gay.

"Their son was gay, and his lover died of AIDS, and now they have lost their son to AIDS," Walter explains. "The husband is now gone, but the wife remains and she is very grateful to have realized that gay people are all right."

Jim and Walter met in July 1959, during the intermission of a performance of *Don Pasquale* in San Francisco. At first, it was a case of mistaken identity.

"I said to my aunt, uncle, and cousin, who had just flown in from Illinois, 'I think I know that fellow from the YMCA,' " Jim recalls. "And I was completely wrong. So I walked up to him and said, 'My name is Jim. What's yours?' And he looked down at me—because he's six-foot-three—and said, 'Walter Nelson-Rees,' and I thought, 'Why give me his middle name?' "

"It was love at first sight," says Walter.

There was an extra seat next to Jim and his family, so Walter joined them for the rest of the show. Afterward the group went out to eat at a deli, Jim dropped off his family at their hotel, and he and Walter took the number six bus to Jim's house at 555 Ortega. The next day Jim's aunt and uncle drove them across the bay to Walter's home in Berkeley.

Jim worked as an accountant and comptroller for a number of firms before retiring with Walter in 1981. Together they opened WIM Fine Arts (W for Walter and IM for Jim), a gallery that sells primarily historical art by California artists.

In their early years as a couple they lived all over San Francisco, the East Bay, and Berkeley before settling into a sixteen-room home in Oakland, where they lived for twenty-four years. But they lost that home in the 1991 brush fire that claimed 3,024 houses.

With most of the couple's possessions destroyed, including hundreds of thousands of dollars of artwork, Jim and Walter moved into the brightly decorated apartment where they now live. It has an amazing kitchen for Walter.

"Walter does the cooking. I do the books," Jim says. "Walter cleans the house. I shop. He doesn't bitch about what I buy and I don't bitch about how he fixes it. He doesn't like to shop. And he's a fantastic cook. It's a wonderful meal three times a day." (Another reason these two would make wonderful grandparents.)

"We don't carry grudges," Walter says, trying to explain why their relationship has lasted so long.

"We believe in each other," Jim adds. "We try to build on each other's strong points. We still like each other . . ."

"We have asked ourselves. But I really have no answer to that question," Walter says. "You enjoy the fact that you have somebody to come home to, somebody to do things with, somebody to converse with."

"*We* *don't understand what kind of role models we are. The thing that amazes us is that*

a number of our young friends are so concerned about having a relationship. . . . it's something that's brand new to us.

We started living together simply because we wanted to live together."

GREG HEYL AND ERIC RILEY

Greg Heyl and Eric Riley are starting over.

For the past fifteen years, they've built a warm, comfortable home in their three-story Brooklyn brownstone. But now they're moving out and preparing to start from scratch in a new home—even though they have no idea what the future holds.

In 1994, Greg was diagnosed with multiple sclerosis, a gradually debilitating disease that would make living in this charming old house with lots of stairs difficult if not impossible. Greg, an emergency-room doctor, thinks a new house renovated for his needs is a pragmatic move.

Eric is more concerned. "It's created stress and worry for me mostly, because I worry for him," he says.

But both men are resigned to letting the future work itself out, just as it did fifteen years ago when they were negotiating the terms of their relationship.

"It's like we've had chapter one, 'Dearly Beloved,' and now we're having chapter two, which is like 'The Wonder Years,' "

Greg says. "I don't wonder about whether we'll stay together in the next fifteen years. I don't worry about that. The wonder comes from the unknown of buying another house and what comes along with that and what happens healthwise to either one of us in the next fifteen years because, God knows, anything can happen. So when I say, 'The Wonder Years,' that's what I mean. The wonder of it all. What will there be in this fifteen?"

The couple met at a disco in Key West in 1980. Greg spotted Eric on the dance floor. "He had a little red leather cap on, like a baseball cap, and little shorts," Greg recalls.

Eric, an actor, lived in New York then; Greg lived in Philadelphia. They courted each other long-distance for the next nine months, then decided to move in together in New York.

At the time Greg was just coming to terms with being gay. He spent much of those first nine months talking with Eric about commitment and careers and the possibility of a lasting relationship in the relatively wild 1980s.

GREG HEYL (RIGHT) AND ERIC RILEY ON A PROMENADE IN BROOKLYN HEIGHTS ALONG THE EAST RIVER.

"*I*t's like we've had chapter one, 'Dearly Beloved,' and now we're having chapter two, which is like 'The Wonder Years.' I don't wonder about whether we'll stay together in the next fifteen years. I don't worry about that. The wonder comes from the unknown of buying another house and what comes along with that and what happens healthwise to either one of us in the next fifteen years because, God knows, anything can happen. What will there be in this fifteen?"

"I had in my mind that I wanted this monogamous relationship. I had gone from woman to man to woman to man, so I had that sexual orientation confusion as well as this whole fear of a gay lifestyle and the promiscuity [stereotype]," Greg says. "I knew that wasn't me. I knew I was gay, but the promiscuity part wasn't a part of me. So it took a long time for me to trust Eric, even though I wanted to."

Eric, who came out and was sexually active with other men at age fifteen, had already figured most of this stuff out. Heterosexual society, he says, "continually tells you to believe in marriage—'Believe in that institution, believe in the fact that you can get together and it will be forevermore and there will be no heartaches. However, if you're homosexual and you're trying to do it, you shouldn't even attempt it because none of you are capable.' And who decided that? Somebody else. So do you believe them, or do you believe in what you do and who you are and try to work it out according to you?"

Eric and Greg decided to work it out for themselves. They married in a very private ceremony ("Just us," Greg says) on December 24, 1980. Their rings speak to their different personalities: Eric wears an intricately carved silver-and-black ring; Greg wears a plain gold band.

"We're happy with our marriage," Greg says. "I don't think it's superficial. I'd be proud to really be able to be married. That would make me happy. I'd like my commitment to be public. I would want everyone to know that I've found a person I'm in love with and making a life and a home with—I want to shout it out."

"It's just natural for us," Eric says. "I have to work to understand him sometimes, but he has to work to understand me, because we are certainly having two different conversations on the same thing. But I find that we agree more than we disagree, which is a big part of being married and being happily married."

In spite of their differences—racial and otherwise—a look around their home makes it clear that the two men have built a perfectly integrated life. On Eric's side of the coat rack there's a Kente cloth scarf, an African print jacket, and various necklaces strung with large and small dark beads. On Greg's side is an array of L. L. Bean-style gear. On the shelves of a curio cabinet, happily sharing space with photos of the couple on ski trips to Aspen or Utah or Sun Valley, there are decades of family photos of smiling black and white people.

But never trust a couple who say they don't work hard at their relationship. After fifteen years they've just become very good at it.

"Figuring out where to go on vacation," Eric says laughing. "That's been the hardest thing. Where did we go and where do we go this time?"

"I don't think there's been anything that's been hard," Greg agrees.

"We miss one another when we're apart," says Eric, whose work has often sent him on long trips with traveling shows. "So I've tried to set up life as much as I can to be here.

" 'I love to come visit you in your sweet home and your sweet life,' a friend of ours says. And it is, you know? I try my best to remind myself of that every day, when I think things are not going well—because usually they never have anything to do with marriage, but everything outside of that—and I can come in here and really get lost in this sweet life." He falls silent for a moment. "But just the move into this new house and everything . . ."

"It's frightening," Greg continues for his husband. "Neither one of us is trying to pretend it's not. But we also, more than that frightening thing, believe that it will be okay. We will not be living like we're living now, but it will be okay."

DAVID HEINZEN AND AARON KAMPFE

David Heinzen and Aaron Kampfe have found their home sweet home on the range.

Well, not exactly.

Most of the time they live in Red Lodge, Montana, "a hamlet," as David calls it. "It's a turn-of-the-century western town that is becoming gentrified," David says. "Aaron and I are the token gay couple everyone invites to dinner. We would never be such a social commodity in a city."

On weekends, though, and often for weeks at a time during the high summer season, Aaron and David live twenty miles away, on a ranch near Roscoe that serves as a destination for their travel business, OutWest Adventures. The company organizes outdoor adventures—hiking, rafting, horseback riding, and so on—for a predominantly gay clientele.

For Aaron, this is home. His family has owned and operated the fifteen thousand-acre Lazy E-L Ranch for more than one hundred years.

"It is spectacular," he says. "If you look out the window you can see twelve thousand-foot peaks, and it's these things that draw people. It's magical. It's more than beautiful—it's unreal. There's no other place like it in the world."

One summer, about a year after they started dating at Boston University, Aaron brought David home to the ranch. Aaron, raised as a cowboy, played ranch hand. David, a music-performance major, spent the summer as ranch cook.

"And I would sneak out of the bunkhouse and sleep with the cook in the cookhouse," Aaron says. "Talk about your butch/femme relationships. We jokingly refer to it as the summer that I was the sissy cowboy and David was the macho houseboy."

A macho houseboy who had grown accustomed to a very urban east-coast environment in Boston. But he got by. "I've always been a very versatile person. I'm the kind of person that rises to a new challenge," David says. "I marvel at the newness of it."

"He really liked making it in the barn," Aaron laughs.

DAVID HEINZEN (LEFT) AND AARON KAMPFE ON THE LAZY E-L RANCH NEAR ROSCOE, MONTANA.

31

"*We didn't have good role models, and society in general doesn't provide a good role model for successful relationships. We had to discover ourselves how to make this relationship work.*"

After college Aaron and David moved out West together. Back in Montana they went through all the typical post-collegiate career uncertainty, wondering what they were supposed to do next. There weren't any great symphony orchestras that would interest or, more importantly, employ David in Missoula, where they lived at the time.

"And that was okay for me," he says. "I was just working as a clerk to pay the bills. We were trying to make a joint decision about a lifestyle for the both of us. We wanted to spend time together doing the stuff we enjoy, and that was creating a strain. It was a difficult time."

Aaron taught high-school English and served after school as drama and debate coach those first two years in Hamilton, about two hours away.

That's when they had the idea for OutWest.

"There wasn't enough time for our relationship," Aaron says, "so we decided we needed a lifestyle change. OutWest gives us more time together, more time for travel, and more time outside."

The idea of working together after living together for seven years gave the couple pause, but only briefly, because they quickly found that their separate talents melded well together.

"It forced us to be better communicators and really appreciate each other's skills and talents," says Aaron. "Planning the meals and running the office—that's not my forte."

"We have clearly defined roles in the company," David says, "but slowly I've been teaching Aaron what I've been doing and we're going to end up learning more than we would have learned on our own."

They've been learning from each other for most of the ten years they've been together. At Boston University, Aaron was an openly gay sophomore when he met David, a senior who was still pretty much in the closet.

"The very next day it seemed as if everything had changed," David says. "I was waiting for someone to open the closet door, and I came bursting out. I met Aaron and never looked back."

But they had to learn how to maintain a solid relationship.

"We didn't have good role models," Aaron says, "and society in general doesn't provide a good role model for successful relationships. We had to discover ourselves how to make this relationship work. I had an ideal in my mind of what kind of relationship I wanted and what I wanted it to look like."

"I never really hung all my hopes or aspirations on having this idea of what a relationship is supposed to be," David says. "I lived my life with Aaron and let it take its own shape."

By the end of a week with David and Aaron on an OutWest adventure, the tour group pretty much knows the story of the tour guide and his trusty cook. And often they say, "You've been together ten years. It must be so easy . . ."

"It's been constant work and constant maintenance," says Aaron. Yet, David adds, "I can look back over the years and see that we've both grown. And then there's that crazy little thing called love."

JIM BENNETT AND DEACON MACCUBBIN

Long before same-sex marriage became a national issue, Jim Bennett and Deacon Maccubbin exchanged vows in a very public ceremony—in front of three hundred and fifty of their closest friends—on February 26, 1982, in Washington, D.C.

Although the setting was right, it wasn't a political statement.

"It was a matter of standing up before friends, associates, and the community at large and pledging our love to each other," Deacon says. "Saying, 'This is a relationship that we want to last, that we want to commit ourselves to, and we want your help in committing to the relationship. We want your support for this relationship.' And so, for all those different reasons and because I was head-over-heels in love, I wanted to do that."

But there had been a delay. Not because of a court injunction or an unwilling church or an uncooperative municipal government (in fact, the mayor sent a commemorative plate to honor the occasion), but because of a reluctant bridegroom—Jim.

"It was tough to say 'I love you,' " says Jim, who was living with a woman in a serious relationship before he met Deacon in 1977. "It was tough to make that commitment because I was still dealing with the straight mentality. I'd come a long way, but when he asked me to marry him, I saw that clearly as a heterosexual ritual I was not going to take part in. If anything, I was getting further away from anything heterosexual to speak of and I didn't feel it was necessary—I thought it was kind of stupid."

Deacon popped the question in 1980, two years after he and Jim started living together.

"I said, 'It's not a joke, and furthermore, there are only two acceptable answers. You can say 'yes' or you can say 'not today.' But 'no' is not an acceptable answer,' " Deacon recalls. "And I said, 'Will you marry me?' And he said, 'Not today.' "

Every day for the next two years Deacon asked the same question and invariably got the same answer. Then Jim started saying "Maybe someday, but not today." Finally while they were visiting friends in Tennessee, Jim said yes—for the second time.

JIM BENNETT (CENTER), DEACON MACCUBBIN (RIGHT), AND JUSTEN BENNETT-MACCUBBIN IN THEIR DUPONT CIRCLE STORE.

"I had asked in the midst of a party at our house, and he said yes, and it went in one ear and out the other. I didn't even hear him," Deacon says.

At their reception, Deacon danced with male city council members who asked him to the floor. And the couple ended their evening in the honeymoon suite of the then brand-new Ramada Renaissance. In fact, they christened the room. Although there were complimentary flowers and champagne, the hotel provided what was perhaps the only glitch of the day—the card delivered with the flowers read, "Congratulations Mr. and Mrs. Maccubbin."

"That didn't go over real well," Jim says, still sounding mildly annoyed.

By the time Deacon and Jim got together, Deacon had become a big deal in the gay community not only as an activist but as the owner of Lambda Rising, one of the first gay bookstore chains in the country.

"If you had told me then that you could make money selling gay books," Deacon says, "I would have laughed."

Now, of course, there are Lambda Rising stores in Baltimore, Rehoboth Beach, Delaware; and Norfolk, Virginia. Their catalog goes out to 650,000 subscribers around the world, and Internet users can access the bookstore through America Online.

When Jim moved to Washington from Maryland, he started working for the store. That made him a part of Deacon's limelit world—whether he wanted to be or not. He wasn't happy about losing his independence.

"I did not want to be controlled," says Jim, who began at Lambda Rising in his early twenties. "I was not used to being controlled at all."

At one fund-raising event, to make a point about his identity,

Jim wrote "Mrs. Maccubbin" on his name tag.

"They knew then that I was a force to be reckoned with," he says. "I have a name. I'm not someone's shadow. I will never, ever be someone's shadow."

Over their twenty years together, Deacon and Jim have had to settle for many compromises as they worked together as partners in the bookstore and in life.

"It's a bit tricky," Jim says, "because we not only are working together, but we also live together. And that's not something I recommend to anyone, and we entered that phase of the relationship with fear and trepidation and also with an agreement that if the work ever interfered with the relationship, the work would end and the relationship would continue."

Deacon adds, "We're together a lot. At home, at work, we're almost constantly together. So, the times on Friday night when he goes out and bowls are a safety valve for both of us. It was difficult in the early years, by the way, to allow that space. I was quite happy being with him twenty-four hours a day, seven days a week."

Deacon considers Lambda Rising his first child. His second is Justen Michael Bennett-Maccubbin. Justen came to live with Deacon and Jim in 1993 as an eighteen year old.

"I always wanted to have a more extended family and never really thought that it would happen," says Deacon. "This was kind of almost the perfect situation—somebody old enough to be able to take care of themselves in many respects, but also young enough and vulnerable enough to need some help and need some guidance and mostly need some love."

The couple first met Justen in St. Louis, where he already had a pretty extraordinary life. Justen was living on his own and had started a gay and lesbian group at Southern Illinois University at

Edwardsville when he was seventeen. He then had dropped out of college and moved to Chicago, where he became the youngest regional delegate to a national gay convention held during Pride Week in D.C. While in the capital, he stayed with Deacon and Jim, and on the eve of his intended return to Chicago he decided he didn't want to go.

When Justen came out to his Mormon family as a teenager his parents were not exactly supportive. His mother rejected the idea, but his father was so angry that he tried to strangle him to death. Justen survived, moved out, and has had no more contact with what he calls "his genetic biological contributors."

"I learn a lot from being in this relationship," Justen now says. "I understand what unconditional love is, I learn what family is, I understand what the holidays are really supposed to be. I mean, they're not supposed to be, like, really super-tense situations where a bunch of people who really don't like each other get together. We're, I think, a stronger family because we're a family of choice as opposed to a family of genetic ties."

He calls Deacon and Jim "Mom" and "Dad" respectively, but lives on his own, not far from his adoptive parents' apartment. All three are anxious to make their relationship official through legal adoption.

"You can't change the world," Deacon says, "but sometimes you can change a little piece of it. This was a case where we felt like we had a chance to do something for one person that would really make a difference in that person's life."

"And we have made a difference," Jim says proudly, his eyes welling up. "It would have been nice to have had my own child. That would have been wonderful. I love kids, but we have Justen, who is our pride and joy. Having Justen with us now is another completion in our lives, you know? It's another closure."

"I always wanted to have a more extended family and never really thought that it would happen. This was kind of almost the perfect situation—somebody old enough to be able to take care of themselves in many respects, but also young enough and vulnerable enough to need some help and need some guidance and mostly need some love."

LYLE DAVIS AND TOM TROENDLE

"It is hard work sometimes, and it's easy for me to decide to do the hard work because the day-to-day is so good," says Tom Troendle of his fourteen-year relationship with Lyle Davis. But, he says, "It's worth the hard work."

"One thing we were very clear on from the very beginning," Lyle adds, "was that this relationship was all about learning. I think our commitment says it's worth the trouble to learn. If there's trouble you don't just bail out."

And, Lyle and Tom say, it takes hard work not just at the beginning of a relationship or in moments of conflict—but all the time. Their home, in a sleepy nook of Fort Lauderdale, Florida, overlooking the New River, is a testament to this belief.

One wall of the couple's living room supports a floor-to-ceiling bookshelf of self-help videos and books on love, relationships, and healing.

"The book we like best, *Getting the Love You Want*, written by Harville Hendrix, is written for heterosexuals, yet everything—across the board—applies to us," Tom says.

As the two men talk about their lives together, they frequently quote a favorite author—usually Hendrix—and pepper their speech with pop-psychology phrases like "recovery" and "transition-clearing" that show they've spent a lot of time doing their homework.

"[M. Scott] Peck says that when you're willing to do the work it's paradoxical—it becomes easier," Tom says. "Just by accepting the fact that it's hard, it becomes easier."

Getting together in the first place was hard work for Lyle and Tom. When they met in a Manhattan nightclub on New Year's night 1983, Tom was already involved in a serious long-term relationship that looked perfect from every angle—at least on the surface.

"We were successful financially, we had a yacht and, I mean, all this *stuff*, and it's hard to get out of that kind of relationship because you feel like you're letting down your friends," Tom says.

LYLE DAVIS (RIGHT) AND TOM TROENDLE IN THEIR BOAT ON THE ATLANTIC OCEAN NEAR FORT LAUDERDALE.

"*One thing we were very clear on from the very beginning was that this relationship was all about learning. I think our commitment says it's worth the trouble to learn. If there's trouble you don't just bail out.*"

"It's the same forces that usually keep heterosexual marriages together. You have to keep up appearances."

In spite of Tom's relationship at the time, he and Lyle wanted to see each other again.

"We both knew that we had a lifelong connection, a lifelong commitment," Lyle says.

In fact, Tom's therapist recommended that he and his then-partner begin seeing other people. They called it "Boys' Night Out." Tom and his partner would divide New York City—one man would get, say, everything west of Broadway, and the other would get everything east of Broadway, to be sure they wouldn't run into each other.

"It was easier than splitting up," Tom says. "Well, it seemed like it would be easier. It's not something I would recommend for making a relationship work."

Tom began seeing Lyle regularly, but when Lyle moved to Los Angeles in 1988, Tom didn't follow.

"I was heartbroken," Lyle says. "I thought I was leaving a relationship behind."

Instead Tom ended his relationship with his then-partner and went to Florida for nine months. There he undertook some of the hard work he and Lyle have come to see as being so important—resolving the final details of his break-up, spending time in serious introspection, and making sure that a new relationship was really the answer he sought.

"I was operating on the assumption that Lyle and I would eventually get together and be lovers," Tom says, "but I had a need to do some transition-clearing so I wouldn't just jump from one relationship to another."

Finally, five years from the day he and Lyle met, Tom moved to Los Angeles to be with Lyle and get serious—but not without more work.

"Once Lyle and I did get together," Tom says, "we did work on intimacy and communication and all those things that are not romantic and are hard to do but make relationships work."

The work continues. The self-help bookshelf tells only part of the story. Lyle and Tom regularly attend workshops, seminars, discussion groups, and lectures on intimacy, communication, making love last, exploring commitment, and other topics that help them explore their feelings and maintain their passion for one another.

"I think both of us have a commitment to ongoing recovery work," Lyle says. "It's not something you do for three years and stop. I mean, at least once a year we go off and do seminars that last a week somewhere. And even though we almost always do that separately, it enhances the relationship."

"I still see friends who love each other very much and are in a good, committed relationship, but the romance dies," Tom says. "They love each other, of course, but I think that the sex dies because they haven't worked through a lot of this stuff. We still have fabulous sex."

"If I didn't have the safety of really knowing Tom loves me, warts and all, even if I'm having a bad day," Lyle continues, "it would be a lot harder to take the risks and get into parts of me that aren't maybe what I think are lovable or appealing. They talk about 'richer and poorer, better and worse,' but a lot of people bail when it gets worse or they're afraid that they won't be loved. I think, for me, one little breakthrough that has evolved over time is just knowing that if I feel crabby I can be crabby and still be loved. On balance it's a lot more fun than it is work.

"And sometimes," he says, "it's magic."

CHRIS HARRISON AND ANDREW PACHO

---

*I*f you're looking for a hunky-dory couple where everything's fine all the time—that's not us," Chris Harrison warns.

He and his lover of six and a half years, Andrew Pacho (but no one calls him Andrew anymore, just Pacho), sit snugly on a sofa in the mirrored living room of their forty-ninth-floor apartment. It's a windy winter's day in midtown Manhattan, and snow and bits of hail and ice are doing somersaults outside their floor-to-ceiling windows.

"All the furniture is on wheels," Chris says, explaining that the living room doubles as a dance studio.

A year after laying the foundation for their personal relationship, Chris and Pacho founded Anti-Gravity, a gymnastics-enhanced troupe of dancers who can just as easily balance on their elbows as their toes. You can see them in print ads, in television commercials, on stage at the Met, or behind the scenes choreographing plays and musicals that require any sort of movement.

Chris and Pacho call their home the anti-gravity apartment.

It's not only their home but also a homebase for Anti-Gravity. A rug in the entry hall catches a breeze and floats above the floor when the windows are open. The cat next door holds the world record for falling forty-nine stories and ending up with less than a scratch. "Sometimes it rains horizontally up here," Pacho says.

"We live and work together," says Chris, "so it's like biting off as much as anybody could possibly bite off to chew, not to mention the fact that we're so much the same in so many ways that very often there are territorial things going on, you know?

"I would never say that relationships are easy. I will say that they're worth it. It's like if you ever want to grow in a spiritual vein, put yourself in a relationship with somebody who's a mirror and look in that mirror every single day and you will grow."

For Chris and Pacho that's less a metaphor than a statement of fact. Chris has fair skin and blue eyes; Pacho has a deeper skin tone, dark curly hair, and deep brown eyes. Yet the two are eerily twinlike. Consider these uncanny similarities: They stand the

CHRIS HARRISON (LEFT) AND ANDREW PACHO DEFY GRAVITY BENEATH THE BROOKLYN BRIDGE.

same height and wear the same size clothes—exactly. Both are from religious families (Mormon and Catholic respectively) and grew up in small cities in the Southwest. Their birthdays? July 9 and July 11—both in 1961. Both were competition-level gymnasts in high school who won scholarships to college. Chris holds a gymnastics world title, and Pacho trained on the national team as an Olympic hopeful. Their mothers can't tell them apart by phone—they share the same vocal range. When Pacho landed the lead role in the New York City Opera's production of *Cinderella*, Chris was his understudy. In 1987, in different countries, at the same time, both played the same role in the musical *Cats*.

"I was singing 'Memory' in Dutch; Chris was in Germany."

". . . *Mondschein, ist ein neues Leben sein . . .*" sings Chris.

"That was so cool," Pacho says.

As they talk they discover even more similarities:

Chris: "Your mother is a hairdresser? You never told me that. Did you know that my mom was a hairdresser?"

Pacho: "Well, I have a lot of secrets and if I gave it all to you at once, you might be bored."

Both men are trained to be competitive, and sometimes that's the hardest part about making their relationship work. They try to maintain separate careers outside of Anti-Gravity. Pacho recently worked on the *King and I* on Broadway with Lou Diamond Phillips and choreographed an opera in Boston while Chris choreographed a Tostitos commercial.

But working on the company—together—early in their relationship cemented a lasting bond. Chris compares it to being a part of any ordinary heterosexual couple: "We were together for a year, had a baby—Anti-Gravity. The baby really took over, and it was screaming and crying, and we had messy diapers and we had to, like, clean up, but who's going to change the diapers? Well,

I guess I'm better at it. I'll do this for a while, and you breast feed it, you know? And sometimes in doing that we lose a little bit of ourselves and our priorities and you forget. You suddenly don't spend enough time with each other."

And then they fight. And make up. "I think what happens is we get to a certain point where things build up and then we have wonderful love-making," Pacho says. "With that, there's a lot of healing."

When they fight, they say, it stems from a desire to make each other and themselves better people—mentally, spiritually, and physically.

"Pacho would say to me, 'I need to be nurtured more,' " Chris says, stroking Pacho's wavy hair. "And I would say back, 'You're not nurturable. I can't nurture you until you are nurturable.' "

"Now I am," Pacho says. "It's one step at a time."

If it means taking a break from each other in separate spaces, they'll do that, too. There's a freedom within their commitment that comes from the fact that neither necessarily expects to be together forever.

"I want to be with Pacho for as long as we are constantly challenging each other and are happy together and growing together," Chris says. "If I put the expectation on us that we will be forever, that's when we start to have trouble."

"Because then love sounds like entrapment," says Pacho.

"Even when we're fighting and it's the worst of times, I know that Pacho loves me unconditionally. There's nothing that I can do that's going to make him totally hate me. He's always standing up for me. This is going to make me cry . . ."—Chris pauses a moment—"And the same with me. I love him just as unconditionally."

Perhaps they're more hunky-dory than they realize.

"*I would never say that relationships are easy. I will say that they're worth it. It's like if you ever want to grow in a spiritual vein, put yourself in a relationship with somebody who's a mirror and look in that mirror every single day and you will grow.*"

MR. BLACKWELL AND R. L. SPENCER

R. L. Spencer is trying to tell the story of how he met Mr. Blackwell.

It's not easy. Partly because Mr. Blackwell is everything you'd imagine Mr. Blackwell to be—at once sophisticated and haughty, salty and charming. David Letterman may get credit for popularizing "Top Ten" lists, but it's Blackwell, an arbiter of fashion and style for nearly four decades, who created and maintains the internationally syndicated, revered and feared annual "Ten Worst Dressed Women List."

They met, Spencer says, at Club Gala, one of the most elegant gay supper clubs in Los Angeles in the late 1940s, where the restaurant Spago is today. "Blackwell had just come out from New York," he says. "In those days he was back and forth between Hollywood and New York. It was one of his trips back to Hollywood. It was a Saturday night."

"A friend introduced us," Blackwell says. "I was with Howard Hughes, and when he dropped my [acting] contract, I hit the beach. I mean, *I hit the beach.* And Spencer was there to pick me up. And he was quiet, and he was kind. I had a need for someone to like me."

"My need was to be needed," Spencer says. "We were pretty young."

"We're not talking age," says Blackwell. "Dates bore me."

In the days after meeting at Club Gala, they went out to dinner a couple of times and talked on the phone constantly. Two weeks later Blackwell moved into Spencer's Benedict Canyon home—right next door to Hollywood's sex symbol *du jour*, Steve Conchran. "Talk about squeaking beds," Blackwell laughs, "Steve's entire house constantly rumbled."

How did they know so quickly that they could make it as a couple?

"We had the same interests . . ." Spencer begins.

"You make a fairy tale out of this and it's going to be boring," Blackwell interjects. "When two people meet there's an intangible

MR. BLACKWELL (RIGHT) AND R. L. SPENCER IN THE ENTRY HALL OF THEIR HANCOCK PARK HOME.

attraction and you don't analyze it. At the beginning there is no plan, there is no future, there is nothing more than the moment."

"You have to have things in common," Spencer continues.

"Excuse me," Blackwell says, "but at the beginning you don't have to have that many things in common. What you have to have in common is a thing called two bedsheets. That's what makes it work those first weeks."

"Well, as he says, the two bedsheets," Spencer agrees with a smile. "But that was only the beginning."

"After the first month," Blackwell says, "a wonderful closeness develops."

"So, the whole thing evolves around that beginning," Spencer says, "and then it grows, you know?"

Their relationship started growing in October 1949. Stonewall was still twenty years away. Gay men gathered in secret, if at all.

Blackwell had yet to become *the* Mr. Blackwell. He had scarcely given up the name he was born with—Richard Selzer—and begun doing bit parts in movies. He had earned some notoriety for appearing semi-nude on Broadway—decades before *Hair* and *Oh, Calcutta!*—in *Catherine Was Great*, a play starring Mae West.

Spencer was doing hair for the rich and famous in Beverly Hills at Saks Fifth Avenue. His clients included Marlene Dietrich, Gracie Allen, Gloria Vanderbilt Sr. and her twin sister Lady Furness, plus most of Hollywood's glamour queens.

Blackwell, who says he's never been in the closet, recalls it as an easy time for two men to meet.

"It wasn't easy," Spencer disagrees.

"We lived in a very closed circuit and the world of being gay was a very tiny world," Blackwell explains. "It survived in its own tiny cocoon. If you ever stepped out of that cocoon, you'd be ostracized."

The couple maintained separate careers until 1958 when they started a clothing business together, the Mr. Blackwell Design Label. The well-known List began in 1960. From the beginning, Spencer managed the business side as Blackwell designed for the American woman and celebrities like Nancy Reagan, Jayne Mansfield, and the Gabor sisters, among others.

"Some of those years were traumatic for both of us—hell on earth," Blackwell says. "We almost lost each other, but Spencer held tight—he was the rock foundation in our relationship. You can't live together and work together, drive downtown together, then go to dinner together, and go to bed together—because you lose all your emotion. You can't do it twenty-four hours a day, every day. You need space—your own space."

But they did it. And have done it for forty-five years. With no regrets.

"How do you stay together?" asks Mr. Blackwell. "Through a lot of tears, screaming, and otherwise. We did the right. We did the wrong. And we did a lot of things that were horrors. But there must be an undercurrent of love that's far deeper. I have loved him for forty-five years. I have not liked him for forty-five years. And he hasn't liked me for a lot of those years.

"But love goes a lot deeper. I mean there's no magic here. This is no Cinderella story. A Cinderella story lasts about seven and a half days. And that little glass slipper manages to break. Someone drops it. That's all. The rest is nothing but a lot of emotional violence, emotional sadness, a lot of emotional need.

"I loved him enough to fight with him," he says finally.

"It hasn't been easy," Spencer says.

So, you were very lucky to find Spencer then, weren't you Mr. Blackwell?

"We were lucky to find each other."

"*H*ow do you stay together? Through a lot of tears, screaming, and otherwise.

We did the right. We did the wrong. And we did a lot of things that were horrors. But there must be

an undercurrent of love that's far deeper. I have loved him for forty-five years."

SHAWN DILLON AND JACK GWINN

T his is my fifth service this year," says a friend of Shawn Dillon's at Shawn's memorial service. "I expect to go to a *few* each year, but not *five*."

Only weeks before, thirty-five-year-old Shawn, who developed AIDS in 1994, was bedridden in his home, trying to overcome a bout with *cryptosporidium*, a virulent intestinal parasite. Nevertheless, he was upbeat, looking toward the future, and anxious to start on a new drug therapy that might extend his life.

"I'm going to be up and about in two weeks," he promised.

Today, at Shawn's memorial service, his husband, Jack Gwinn, finds that words are insufficient to express his sense of loss, to celebrate Shawn's life and the couple's love for each other. Instead he turns to music—a men's chorus, accompanied by a piano, performs moving songs of love and longing throughout the service.

"Music is always a part of my life," says Jack after the service. "And I think that was the easiest way for me to give a really nice tribute to Shawn."

Shawn, too, loved music. Family and friends remember him fondly as the men's chorus member who couldn't always carry a tune. They also speak of his amazing potato-leek soup, cranberry bread, barbecue ribs, and dinners—"for four"—that could feed an entire neighborhood.

It is an emotional afternoon. Shawn's death has caught everyone who knew him by surprise. His doctor had just begun administering a protein drip intended to boost Shawn's weight. And just two months earlier, Jack says, he and Shawn were planning a trip to the west coast and thinking aloud: "Five years from now we'll do this and that . . ."

"It was a major shock," Jack says. "But he [died] at home, in his sleep. As strong as his will to live was, he couldn't control his life anymore. His body was too weak."

Jack and Shawn's relationship could have withstood almost anything else—and it did. The two men shared their thoughts on this a few weeks before Shawn's death . . .

SHAWN DILLON (LEFT) AND JACK GWINN ALONG THE DELAWARE RIVER WHERE THEY USED TO WALK TOGETHER.

"*You just don't give up. You grind in your heels and do what you have to do.*"

When they first met, "it was a rotten, rotten time," Shawn recalls.

In a series of bizarre conflicts with the jealous son of a closeted employer, Shawn had lost his house, his car, and his job all around the same time. And yet Jack did not lose confidence in him. Nor did Shawn lose hope about his relationship with Jack.

"I had this mind-set then that I would meet this nice man and settle down, and Jack happened to be in the way," Shawn says.

After a year of dating, the couple settled into a house in Princeton, New Jersey. Things went smoothly until Shawn's parents divorced, and his mother underwent a religious "awakening" that made her hostile toward his relationship with Jack.

"She went so far as to write him a letter saying he was living with the devil," Jack says. "I thought, 'Well, I'm the only one here.' "

The next crisis for the couple came when Jack almost went to jail. While working for a bank, he had practiced what he likes to call "creative bookkeeping," adding upwards of ten thousand imaginary dollars to his bank account.

"I wasn't taking money out of people's accounts," he explains, "I was just making mine bigger—creating more zeroes."

When the bank caught on, Jack's supervisors were angry, of course. They were also amazed. Jack had found a way to rip off the bank that no one had thought of before. His lawyer told him that he was looking at six months in jail and would have to pay the money back. Jack was sure Shawn would leave him, but he didn't.

"You just don't give up," Shawn says. "You grind in your heels and do what you have to do. We both worked, like, two jobs. We lucked out."

Before the trial, Jack's prospects didn't look good, but the prosecution would have a hard time proving him a hardened white-collar criminal.

"I had nothing to show for the money," he explains. "I had no car, no stereo, no CDs. I was giving money to friends. It was basically a lot of goodwill stuff with money that wasn't mine."

And then Jack got a lucky break. A member of his barber-shop quartet stood up for him in the judge's chamber—the magistrate also sang in a quartet—and Jack ended up with three years' probation.

The couple moved to Beverly, New Jersey, and started from scratch, launching a telephone answering service together. The work was demanding and consumed most of their time. Shawn's interest in Jack began to wane, and he moved out for three months.

"We didn't seem to have much in common for a while," he recalls.

"He wouldn't tell me why he needed to go," says Jack. "The first month I was totally depressed."

Eventually Jack started dating another man. His new friend happened to be at the house one day when Shawn came home to get something out of his closet.

It was this surprise meeting that brought Shawn to his senses. "This is my husband, and I'm not ready to give up," he told himself.

Jack and Shawn got back together, but their trials weren't over. In 1990, they decided to get complete physicals—including an HIV test. They received their results together: Shawn had better cholesterol than Jack; Jack had better blood pressure than Shawn; Jack was HIV-negative.

"And then the doctor goes, 'You're HIV-positive,' to Shawn," says Jack. "It was such a shock to hear that. But I think that the fact that he had left me before made me strong and I was able to deal with this. We were just going to go on with our life."

But life doesn't always play fair.

"I was spared the trauma of the disease," Jack says today, as friends mill around him to offer their comfort. He fingers the wedding band on his left hand—it's extra wide now because he has welded Shawn's ring to his.

"He spared me that really ugly part. He was at home. He was with me. It was exactly how he wanted to go—just five years sooner than planned."

TOM BIANCHI AND MARK PRUNTY

*I*n 1988, Tom Bianchi lost his on-and-off (but mostly on) lover of twelve years to AIDS. The loss was devastating but it was made worse, Tom says, by his mother's nonchalant reaction. When he called to tell her of David's death, she said, "Well, I'm sorry to hear that. And oh, let me tell you about your grandmother . . ."

Seven years later Tom called his mother to tell her how that had felt. If David had been a woman, he explained, his mother would have said, "We'll be on the next plane." It was a painful conversation, but Tom says his mother now understands his relationships are just as valid as his siblings' heterosexual ones.

When David died, Tom figured that was it as far as his life's major love affairs were concerned. "I thought, 'I had the grand passion. A lot of people don't get a chance to have this.' And I had no expectations about the future."

But three years later, at a publication party for Tom's book *Out of the Studio*, a friend introduced him to a very attractive young man named Mark Prunty. Mark had modeled for other photographers and knew some of the models who had worked with Tom.

"They said he was a wonderful man," Mark says, "and he turned out to be a *very* wonderful man."

In those hazy, romantic moments after their first date Tom held Mark's head in his hands and said, "I've found you."

"I recognized him," Tom says. "I recognized him."

"We had been together before," Mark says. "Most definitely."

Later, Tom showed Mark a pencil drawing a close friend had done from a snapshot of Tom as a little boy. The drawing was unframed. Mark borrowed it and returned it a week later.

"It came back beautifully framed like that," Tom says, pointing to the small drawing that sits among his own paintings and photos in the couple's earth-toned condo. "And I thought, 'Oh my God. This is certainly more intimate than, you know, a dozen roses.' I was enormously impressed by that act. This was not an ordinary date."

Mark knew exactly what he was doing. He had decided, he

TOM BIANCHI (RIGHT) AND MARK PRUNTY BY A HOLYWOOD POOL TOM USES AS A SETTING FOR MANY OF HIS PHOTOGRAPHS.

57

says, that Tom "is a wonderful man and somebody needs to take care of him. I'll do it very nicely. It was like our souls just met. It was very easy right at first." Until they started to work together.

After a ten-year career as a lawyer for Columbia Pictures and another ten years as a painter-sculptor, Tom was emerging as one of the finest black-and-white photographers of the male nude. In the early 1990s Mark became his trusty and dedicated darkroom assistant, selecting images and printing the final photos. Mark also began to handle the business side of Tom's life—at least that was the idea.

"I had this fantasy that Mark was going to be this fabulous astute business person who was going to organize all that stuff so I could go off into the world and be an artist," Tom says. Then, turning to Mark, he asks, "What was your fantasy?"

"The same," Mark responds. "That I would enjoy doing that. It wasn't what I wanted to do. I wanted to be creative too. That's what drew me to Tom so much—the creativity and the beauty of what he captured. And when I was doing the business side it just wasn't me."

So in May of 1996 Mark took his own job as a graphic artist for the Los Angeles-based *Provocateur* magazine.

"We're very much individuals now; when we came into the relationship we were working as one. That's what a relationship is about—" Mark says, reclining back on the unfolded futon that serves as the couple's living room couch, "growing and changing."

When Mark began his new job, Tom also began a new project—he helped found CytoDyn, a biotechnology research firm that's working on developing a nontoxic AIDS therapy. Tom has a personal as well as financial investment in the firm because he credits CytoDyn's treatment with saving his life in 1993.

"There was a period of time when I didn't think I would be around much longer," Tom says. "I remember a specific night that was really an epiphany, because Mark turned to me that night and said, 'I know you're leaving, but I'm waiting here for you forever to come back.' And that helped me identify how sick I had gotten. I was one of those people they expected not to be around in a few months."

"I have never thought since I met Tom that he was going to die of HIV," says Mark, who is HIV-negative. "When I saw him getting sick I knew he wasn't taking care of himself. I said, 'Go to the gym.' "

And now finding a treatment or cure for AIDS is the focus of Tom's business life. He uses the advances from his publishers to cover the costs of photographic materials for his books but donates the rest of his royalties to CytoDyn. Meanwhile, the focus of his personal life is acknowledging how fortunate he is to have experienced for a second time a grand, passionate love.

"From time to time we just sit down and remind ourselves how much—*how much*—is wonderful," Tom says. But he points out that even in the midst of such serious conversations about their relationship and their lives, he and Mark feel it's important to keep things in perspective—to be able to laugh at themselves from time to time.

"Once," Tom says, "we were having a very serious and intimate discussion, and our cat, Marky, climbed up my shoulders and his paws were on my head and he was licking my hair into little cowlicks, which was making me look very Clarabelle Cow-ish, and . . ."

". . . and Tom's sitting on the edge of the bed being very stern and serious with me," says Mark, picking up the story, "and I'm dying to laugh and I said, 'I can't take you seriously. You have a cat standing on your shoulders licking your head.' "

"That," says Tom, "is what a good marriage is about."

"*W*e're very much

individuals now; when

we came into the relationship

we were working as one.

That's what a relationship

is about—growing

and changing"

TIM CASS AND RAYMOND DRAGON

Raymond Dragon has always gone after what he wants. And when the former competitive gymnast with an engineering degree, dance training, and early careers as a model and fashion designer for WilliWear sets his mind to something, he usually succeeds. This is the guy who single-handedly built an entire men's clothing line around a clingy yet comfortable bicycle short.

In 1990, he launched Raymond Dragon menswear with a factory in the garment district and, eventually, a retail store across the street from Barneys. The store would be the first of several. Located in Manhattan's Chelsea neighborhood, it attracted the gay consumers who would become Ray's core customers. Today his slinky clothes and swimwear, designed for bodies beautiful, have become required party wear on Fire Island, South Beach, and anywhere else men spend too much time and energy on their bodies to keep them covered up.

So when Ray decided to go after Tim Cass seven years ago, Tim didn't really stand a chance.

"He just came up to me," Tim says, "embraced me, and kissed me."

Ray recalls being more demure when they met at a house party on Fire Island during the summer of 1989.

"We were lying on deck chairs, and he was in the chair next to me, and we had been there a long time," he says. "I got up and went over and lay on top of him. That's what I remember."

It turned out to be a great summer on the island for both men, even though neither was interested in starting a relationship immediately.

"You don't get married at the beginning of summer," says Ray, who ended up with an entire house to himself on the island a couple of weekends later and needed some company.

"It was the first time I met Spike," says Tim, referring to Ray's Chihuahua.

Ray and Tim closed out the summer at the annual Gay Men's Health Crisis Morning Party—together.

TIM CASS (LEFT) AND RAYMOND DRAGON IN THE WINDOW OF RAY'S CHELSEA STORE.

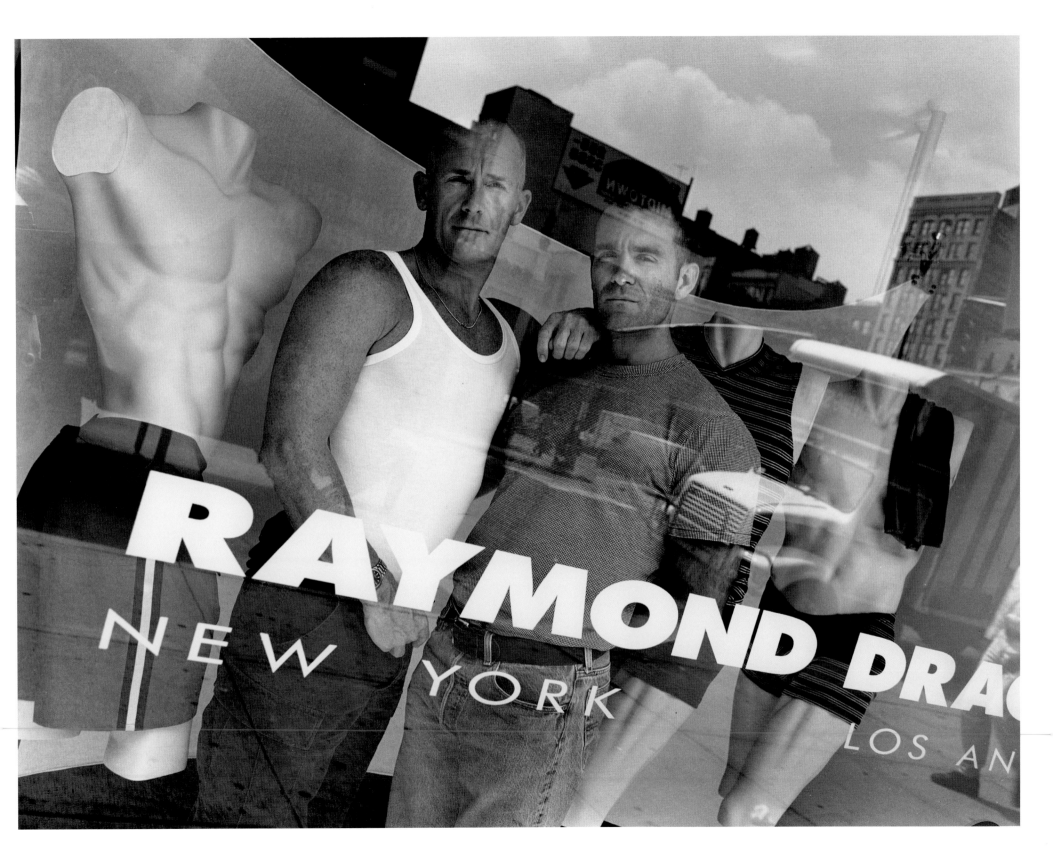

"*I think couples break up so often because they spend so much time together, like nagging each other to death.*"

"That's what I consider to be our anniversary," says Tim, "because it was the first time we went somewhere together and left together."

The two men moved in together the following spring—and promptly stopped seeing each other.

For the first few years of their relationship, Ray was consumed with launching his company. He spent most of every single day—as he still does—at his studio, managing his wholesale business. Tim, who now manages Ray's store in New York, then worked five nights a week as a waiter and bartender.

"Our initial schedules didn't allow us much time together, so it was really easy to have a relationship," says Ray. (He laughs as he says this, but he isn't kidding.) "I think couples break up so often because they spend so much time together, like nagging each other to death."

Both men say their time living separate lives in one house was probably the best thing for their relationship.

"It stopped us from getting tired of each other," Tim says. "We didn't have the opportunity to get used to each other."

Once Ray had established his successful wholesale business and factory, producing not only his line for sale nationwide, but also samples and fashion show pieces for the likes of Donna Karan, he began to entertain the idea of a retail store. Tim, a professional architect with an eye for industrial design and marketing would be an invaluable resource. But Ray had tried to share a company with a lover once before, and it hadn't worked—not for the business or the relationship. He was concerned about making that mistake again.

"But [Ray and his ex] worked together on a day-to-day level," Tim says, "whereas the way we're set up, I'm at the store and I can control what goes on there, and Ray's at the studio, so . . ."

"We have a nice amount of distance between us," interrupts Ray.

It's stressful but not unmanageable, they say. With a growing business that needs all of their attention, there's no time to sneak off to Fire Island—or even Coney Island—for an afternoon. No short trips to South Beach for some sun. Even social events or dinner at restaurants don't really qualify as downtime.

"Wherever we go, there are always people," Tim says, without a hint of complaint in his roguish Australian accent. "And people mean that you have to be 'on' because they know us and recognize us, so it's very hard to escape from the business."

That should make living together nearly impossible, yet somehow it's not.

"It's been surprisingly easy," Tim continues, "which makes us think that it's meant to be—that we are together—because it just feels right. There aren't the conflicts, the disputes that I've had in previous relationships."

"I think people go into relationships with a lot of ideas, a lot of wants, and, you know, you can't have those things. You gotta go in and expect nothing and then be really grateful for what you get," Ray says.

And what he's got is *exactly* what he wants.

JOHN BELL AND PETE SMITH

Pete Smith joined the Royal Navy when he was sixteen because he loved the sea. He left it fourteen years later because he loved John Bell.

They met at a party Pete crashed in Earl's Court, then London's gay district, in 1968. They began a relationship that was a secret "as far as the military was concerned," says Pete, now fifty-seven. Eventually John moved to Portsmouth to be near Pete's base.

About the same time, a fellow soldier was caught sleeping with another man, and the military brass decided to court-martial him, but not before asking him to name other gay seamen. There is no such thing as "don't ask, don't tell" in the U.K., so when his superiors asked, Pete told. "I think they were taken aback because they expected me to deny it," he says.

John, reclining on a love seat, still has the taste of sour grapes in his mouth. "Don't they realize there are bloody homosexuals in the military by now?"

Pete was discharged in 1970 and now works for an electronics firm. His love of the sea continues, though. Maritime artifacts and paintings of regal sailing ships fill the couple's dining room. John works as a sales manager for an industrial clothing supplier. He and Pete share the mortgage on their modest two-story house in Luton, thirty miles north of London. It's also home to their dog (Emma) and two cats (Kevin and Oliver). Redouté botanical prints line the stairway, and Pete and John have a growing collection of art deco and art noveau bronze sculptures that includes reproductions of works by Chiparus.

To borrow from naval parlance, Pete and John say their relationship has been smooth sailing ever since they met. "We never actually considered anything else did we?" John, forty-eight, asks his burly teddy bear of a partner. "Not any alternative. Everything worked."

Did they expect to make it this far?

"Well no," John says, "But then again we never thought that we wouldn't, either. Did we?"

JOHN BELL (LEFT) AND PETE SMITH IN LONDON'S EARL'S COURT, WHERE THEY MET IN 1968.

JEFF OAKES AND JEFF SIDELL

As a young boy Jeff Sidell's most cherished, recurring fantasy was to have a husband.

"I wanted that so badly," he says. "I'm very much the nesting type."

Jeff Oakes, who's lived with Sidell almost since the day they met twelve years ago, is also the nesting type. The couple met in college at a friend's birthday party.

"It was a set-up," Oakes explains. "The host saved the seat next to me for Jeff, who was late."

Here, Sidell picks up the story. "The host cornered me in the vestibule and said, 'I invited Jeff Oakes here especially for you. Now you go sit next him.' And I walked into the living room and I was like, 'Wow! This is great.' I fell head over heels in love with him."

That was September 1985. They had moved in together by Thanksgiving.

"Jeff was twenty-two and I was going to turn twenty-five," says Oakes, now thirty-seven. "We didn't have any money, and it was stupid to pay two rents since we were spending so much time together."

Sidell agrees that if they had been older it never would have happened the same way. "I don't remember having thought 'Gee, this is a big step,' or 'This is something I should be thinking about,'" he says.

"We were naive. Neither of us knew that the other person wasn't totally insane," Oakes says. "We were lucky."

The Jeffs (their friends call them "Big Jeff" and "Little Jeff") spent a year living together in Hanover, New Hampshire, where Sidell ("Little Jeff") worked for a software company, and Oakes worked as a carpenter restoring eighteenth-century homes. Then one day, on a drive through the Connecticut River Valley, they spotted a farmhouse in Vermont that would change their lives.

"I said 'Jeff, we have to have this house,'" Oakes recalls.

Sidell, being the more rational one (sort of) insisted on

JEFF OAKES (RIGHT) AND JEFF SIDELL IN BERKELEY MARINA PARK, ACROSS THE BAY FROM SAN FRANCISCO.

"We were naive. Neither of us knew that the other person wasn't totally insane. We were lucky."

checking out a few other properties first, just to go through the motions of comparison shopping.

"We ended up getting the house," says Oakes. "And then we moved in and we were like, 'What have we done? We don't know who our neighbors are! Are we going to get crucified here?' "

The purchase of a new home was the occasion for a visit from Sidell's parents. "That was the first time my parents visited me and Jeff," Sidell says, "and he very quickly became part of the family."

This was a realization of Oakes's long-standing fantasy. "I wanted stability and love and to be a part of someone who was connected and part of something that was bigger," he says. "Becoming a part of Jeff's family has been a real blessing for me."

The relationship with Sidell's parents became very close. When the Jeffs traveled to Europe to celebrate their tenth anniversary, Sidell's parents toured Italy with them.

"Jeff really made an effort to involve my parents and to be a part of their lives and bring them into our lives," Sidell says. "I don't know that I would be so much a part of that if he hadn't done it. I'm glad that it happened."

One night at a neighboring farmhouse, a psychic from New York did a palm reading for the Jeffs and declared that this was their third life together.

"We looked at each other," Oakes recalls, "and said, 'Let's get it right this time.' [The psychic] also said we wouldn't be in Vermont in two years. And we were like, 'We have two dogs and twelve cats and we've been spending all this time trying to keep this house standing . . .'"

"But he was right," Sidell says.

A year later they moved west for graduate school. For three years they lived three hours apart while attending separate uni-versities—Oakes was in St. Louis; Sidell was in Urbana, Illinois.

Oakes had hoped to become a doctor but bombed the MCAT exams. Sidell, whose father and brother are both doctors, convinced him to consider something else.

"I told him that even though I thought he would make a very good doctor that wasn't really where his talents lie," Sidell says. "It was clear to me his real talent was for design."

"It made me snap out of it and decide what was really important to me," Oakes says. "I took the risk and applied to a design program." Today he works for a firm that develops and builds better nurses' stations and hospital environments.

The couple completed their master's degrees at the same time. Sidell applied to a doctoral program in computer science at the University of California at Berkeley, and he and Oakes moved to California four years ago.

"And we're sure that we're going to live here the rest of our lives," says Sidell. "It's the coolest place we ever lived."

"It's a pretty special place to live," Oakes agrees. "[Sexuality] is really not an issue. What's important [to people here] is what you do, not who you sleep with.

"It's taken me a good ten years to say, 'Yeah, it doesn't matter,' " he continues. "When I met Jeff I was still really uncomfortable about all of that, and by observing Jeff and how he moved through life and situations . . . slowly but surely . . ."

He would like his relationship with Sidell to be a model for others—to friends' children, to his and Sidell's nephews and nieces, to other gay people, and especially to any young boys out there who might also be dreaming of finding a husband. "I feel like we're ordinary guys," he says, "who could be role models for a younger generation and show them that it's possible to have a long-term, loving relationship."

CARL HOUSE AND HENRY MESSER

We don't have any secrets," says Henry Messer of Carl House, his partner of forty-six years.

"You get used to each other after a while," Carl adds. "At this point we're just growing old together."

They met in 1951. Henry was a surgeon at Maxwell Air Force Base in Montgomery, Alabama. Carl was in the Army, stationed one hundred miles away at Camp Rucker. Every weekend he hitchhiked to see Henry. Of course, their courtship was anything but open.

"The military was really out to catch homos," Henry says. "It was their most important mission in life. It seemed more important to many of them than fighting the [Korean] War. It was all-encompassing."

Nevertheless, Carl says, "I learned how extensive the gay world was when I met [other gay soldiers] in the Army."

It was a fellow soldier who brought about Henry's discharge. "A guy stole my wallet with all my identification in it," he explains. The military police caught the thief. In an effort to shift attention from his crime, he revealed he'd had had sex with Henry. "It was almost as big a deal as winning the [Second World] War," Henry recalls. "The inquisitors were very, very sharp. They could get almost anything out of anybody."

They searched Henry's barracks, examined the film in his camera, read the letters in his desk, and confiscated his address book. At the end of the investigation, Henry resigned—just short of completing his two-year enlistment.

During the search of Henry's room, investigators discovered a letter from Carl. They tracked him down, too, but "It didn't go any further because I kept my mouth shut," Carl says.

When Carl completed his service, he and Henry were anxious to put the military behind them. They moved to New York City so Henry could begin his residency at St. Vincent's Hospital. Carl found work at a car dealer, then went to school to become a medical lab technician, then he took up the management of the

CARL HOUSE (LEFT) AND HENRY MESSER OUTSIDE THE DETROIT INSTITUTE OF ARTS.

"*The military was really out to catch homos. It was their most important mission in life. It seemed more important to many of them than fighting the war. It was all-encompassing.*"

couple's property in the city. "He became a landlady," Henry jokes.

It was 1955. New York was a Mecca for young people who wanted to live their lives their own way. It was particularly attractive to young gays and lesbians who had discovered they weren't alone while serving in World War II. When the war ended, they went to the city rather than return to the isolation of small-town America.

"There was a golden age in the 1920s and then another in the 1950s," Henry says, pointing out that both were post-war eras.

"There was lots of theater; lots of activity," Carl continues. "We were young—there were lots of parties."

"We would go out for a walk and there would be a street party. Nothing's like that anymore," Henry laments.

As that golden age began to fade in the mid-1960s, Henry became involved in the Mattachine Society, one of the first "homophile" organizations that attempted to bring about social change on homosexual issues. "It was the first kind of meeting of gay people that wasn't cruising in bars," Henry says. "Looking back on it, it all seems kind of stupid. A straight psychologist would come in and talk about what it means to be gay—in those days that was very radical."

Henry says he joined the group because, at the time, the NYPD blue were beginning to raid bars and harass gays on the street.

Carl followed Henry reluctantly—"As a dutiful mate," he says. "I'm not an activist. He was always the one leading the charge."

Henry says those turbulent years leading up to Stonewall in 1969 mark his official coming out. "It probably happened over a period of twenty years," he says.

"A lot of people knew we were gay," Carl says. "It was obvious what our relationship was . . ."

"If they didn't know," Henry interjects, "they were stupid."

Henry's parents certainly knew. But they never accepted his sexuality or his relationship with Carl.

"They would have always preferred something else," Carl says sadly. "I think a lot of heterosexuals go through the same thing. Parents are the ones that pull the strings, and it wasn't easy, but I lived through it. It could have been nicer."

Henry's parents excluded Carl from family gatherings, so eventually Henry stopped going. "His father called me a couple of times practically weeping," Carl says. "And he would ask could I please help them get back together."

"But still not inviting Carl to their home," Henry notes. "They had forty years to change, and he could have worked on it. Not a bit was resolved before he died."

"You can't change people sometimes," Carl says.

But change continues to be one of Henry's goals. Today he and Carl live in Detroit. Henry, now seventy, is a member of a local gay political action group, the Triangle Foundation. "For me it's a mission," he says. "There's still harassment and discrimination. There were quite a few anti-gay murders in Michigan last year, but we can call up the Chief of Police in Detroit and go meet with him and the mayor and city council. That was certainly not the way it was back in the 1960s."

Henry retired ten years ago from his position as chief of neurosurgery at Wayne County General Hospital. Carl, now sixty-eight, stopped working in 1976 to "loaf," which to him means concentrating on the couple's home and his interests in classic cars and ocean liners.

After weathering forty-six years of progress and setbacks in gay liberation together, both men agree that things are moving in the right direction—but not fast enough, Henry says. "I'm hoping I can make things better than they are," he explains.

"I think you have," says Carl with quiet admiration.

THATCHER BAILEY AND CHRISTOPHER MALARKEY

Thatcher Bailey and Christopher Malarkey have been given a second chance.

"I'm one of those folks who's back in life, back in the work force," says Thatcher, still HIV-positive but undergoing treatment with the latest weapon in the battle against AIDS.

Thatcher was only thirty-nine when he retired from his job in 1993. By 1995 his health had started to fade, and it seemed the end was near.

"I was very much preparing to get sick and die," he says.

Then, in the nick of time, science offered a life raft—a cocktail of several drugs, including protease inhibitors and anti-retrovirals, that appears to neutralize the effects of HIV and boost production of T-cells in some people.

"Almost immediately my health began to improve," Thatcher says. "It's a remarkable thing."

"Just a few months ago," says Christopher, "I thought that death was a possibility for Thatcher, and now I don't feel that way."

The two men first met through their respective boyfriends, who were best friends. Their boyfriends both had AIDS and would eventually lose their lives to the illness. Thatcher took the loss of his lover, Frank, particularly hard—it was the end of a serious ten-year relationship that he calls the most important one of his adult life.

"I was in that relationship from twenty-five to thirty-five," he says. "I would compare this relationship to that relationship, which was unfair, and happily Christopher bore through that."

Frank's death also served as a wake-up call to his and Thatcher's circle of friends. Seattle is what is called a second-wave AIDS city. It's a cycle behind New York, San Francisco, and other cities that suffered their most catastrophic losses to the disease in the 1980s. Gay communities in Seattle and cities like it suffered devastating losses a decade later.

"When Frank died," Thatcher says. "He was one of the first to touch us all. It was hard for our group of friends."

THATCHER BAILEY (LEFT) AND CHRISTOPHER MALARKEY ON SEATTLE'S PUGET SOUND FERRY.

In the summer of 1990 Christopher and Thatcher met again at Seattle's Goodwill Games. Christopher, known affectionately as "Topher," was working with a gay and lesbian theater company; Thatcher was helping organize a demonstration against the National Endowment for the Arts.

"I had always thought Topher was attractive," Thatcher says. "We hooked up there and got smitten and began a long and rich and rocky romance."

Really rocky, Christopher explains.

"We dated for six months and then broke up for six months, and then we dated for three months and got back together and then broke up for two months, and then we got back together and decided to get married," he says. "It was getting a little old for people."

Thatcher thinks they may have decided to get married for the wrong reasons—just to end the cycle of getting together and breaking up. But with time, their marriage has turned into something more solid.

"We were ambivalent when we were doing the ceremony because there was some conversation about selling out and mimicking heterosexual standards," he says. "The fact that our families embraced it made us kind of nervous. But it allowed us to make a commitment that has been a rock for us."

With the return of Thatcher's health, the two men are facing the prospect that their rock may have to weather many more years of commitment than they previously expected.

"It seems so recent that I can't even give a perspective on it," Christopher says, struggling to find the words.

"It's just refreshing not to have this specter of imminent demise over your head," Thatcher says.

"Flippantly, I would say that there were things that I thought I would put up with that I'm not going to put up with anymore," Christopher says. "I can't really tell you what's different about it. I mean, each day is different."

Their future, which once seemed so clear, has suddenly become rather hazy. Christopher says he's thinking seriously about the next twenty or thirty years. He wants to save money, maybe open a retirement account.

"It's very difficult to keep conflicting possibilities in your head—'I might die/I'm going to live forever,' " says Thatcher. "It was a challenge for our relationship. Now we're going to be together longer than we thought we would."

"*We were ambivalent when we were doing the ceremony because there*

was some conversation about selling out and mimicking heterosexual standards.

The fact that our families embraced it made us kind of nervous."

JOHN WHYTE AND TOM WILSON WEINBERG

They met cute—on a train platform at Philadelphia's 30th Street Station in November 1973.

"I was going to a medical-school interview in Brooklyn, and Tom was going to the theater with a friend," says John Whyte of Tom Wilson Weinberg, his partner of twenty-five years. "And we eyed each other starting at 30th Street and ending at Penn Station with an exchange of phone numbers."

It was the beginning of a nine-month long-distance relationship. Finally, instead of Brooklyn, John decided on a medical school in Philadelphia and moved in with Tom.

"It was a little bit scary," John recalls. "We had never been together for more than a couple of days at a time. It was a pretty big risk. Why does one do those things? It was just an impulse."

Tom says part of the initial attraction was their joint interest in gay activism. John, who had just come out and joined the gay movement, used to meet men—mostly closeted—who would ridicule his political ideas because they weren't interested in being activists. With Tom, who was just starting to be completely open himself, that didn't happen.

"We were starting our relationship just at the point where I was coming out politically," says Tom, formerly director of a boys' camp in Maine, where his job had forced him to stay in the closet. "I had been out sexually and socially for a number years, but I decided that I wanted to be more open and politically active so I resigned from that job, moved to Philadelphia, and became involved in some political stuff."

In Philadelphia, Tom founded Giovanni's Room—a gay and lesbian bookstore—with a couple of friends. They also started the now defunct *Philadelphia Weekly Gazette*. Today he uses his activist energy to fuel his work as a songwriter. He's written musical reviews that have played off-Broadway and around the country. He calls his music satirical, gay political humor. He also writes choral pieces for "the huge number of gay and lesbian choruses cities have now."

JOHN WHYTE (LEFT) AND TOM WILSON-WEINBERG IN PHILADELPHIA'S RITTENHOUSE SQUARE.

*"*I *t was a little*

bit scary. We had

never been together for

more than a couple

of days at a time.

It was a pretty big risk.

Why does one do

those things? It was

just an impulse."

John, whose work has moved the couple to Minneapolis, then Boston, then back to Philadelphia, is more of a homebody. When he and Tom first moved in together, John wanted to have children almost immediately. "I was looking for a way to adopt or have a surrogate mother or do something that would give us a child," he says.

"And I was not," replies Tom, flatly.

To complicate matters, several lesbian couples and single women approached the couple over the years as potential fathers for their children. Tom mostly resisted.

"In the 80s, we talked about it with each other, but said no when we were approached because we didn't want to make that commitment," he says. "I never really saw myself as a parent."

While they were living in Boston, however, they became friendly with another lesbian couple who eventually asked if one of the men would father a child with them. The offer was especially appealing because the women wanted to assume all primary care and decision making for the child.

Once again John and Tom said no, though they thought about it more seriously this time. Their hesitation was not so much about becoming parents, but about HIV—neither man knew his status.

"We couldn't make a commitment without knowing that," says Tom. "When we moved back to Philadelphia we remained interested. We decided to get tested."

"We had thought about it on and off for years, and typically my role would be to bring it up and Tom's role would be to ultimately not want to do it," John says.

This time it was different. With negative HIV test results in hand, they began the process with the two women back in Boston.

"We got a lawyer, they got a lawyer," says Tom. "It was kind of strange because it was like negotiating a divorce contract."

Over the course of nine months, as all of the legal issues were resolved, they decided John should be the sperm donor because he was the most enthusiastic about being a father.

"Now we have two babies," Tom says happily, "and these are the most planned children the world has ever known."

They have a four-year-old daughter and a two-year-old son. Initially, they planned only one child, but as their daughter neared her second birthday, her moms began to think she needed a sibling.

"Again, I was the reluctant one," Tom says, "but I think part of the reasoning [that changed my mind] was that in this unconventional family, who knows what they would have to deal with on their own? This way they would have each other as full brother and sister."

John and Tom spend most of their summers and vacations in a one-room cabin in Maine. It sits in a lush green cul-de-sac on a lake. They are probably the only gay couple in the area. They were always invited to take part in the straight summer social scene—potlucks and cookouts and get-togethers—but no one ever discussed their relationship until John and Tom started talking about their children.

"They really related to that in a big way," says Tom, growing misty-eyed. "Now they are seeing our kids grow up. When we told our neighbors who was coming for the first time, the immediate response was, 'It's a potluck!' It's fantastic."

The children spend most of their time with their mothers in Boston but see their fathers nearly every weekend, making regular trips to Philadelphia.

"The kids are terrific," says John, a proud dad. "They're interesting and funny and out-of-control."

But the proudest parent may be Tom. "I'm probably still the least comfortable as a parent," he admits, "but I love meeting them for Gay Pride events. We all walk up Fifth Avenue as a family."

LEONARD GREEN AND STEVE LANGLEY

To many gay men, Leonard Green is the ultimate in contradictions. He's black and Republican; he's also ultra-conservative and gay. He's opposed to the federal gay civil rights bill but hopes one day to legally marry his partner of nine years, Steve Langley—who defines himself as a left-leaning moderate.

But Leonard doesn't see these things as contradictions. And he points out that he's not alone.

"People who were gay gave money to Bush," he says. "People who were gay gave money to Reagan. People who were gay gave money to Buchanan. People who were gay gave money to David Duke."

"I've learned that just because I love him doesn't mean everyone else is going to," says Steve with a gesture of resignation. "There are times that I feel like Pat Nixon."

At the Pink Teacup in Greenwich Village over brunch, Leonard, decidedly humorless, launches into a diatribe about abortion that culminates with the Republican party's unyielding conditions for when it should be legal: only in cases of incest, the endangerment of the mother's life, and rape.

"Because raped life isn't life?" pipes in a woman from the next table. She and Leonard debate the issue for a good fifteen minutes, drawing the ire and attention of two women on the other side of our table.

Meanwhile, Steve pays attention only to his pancakes.

Leonard grew up in New Orleans with eleven siblings. His mother referred to gay men as "stinky things," but two of his brothers also were gay. One came out at fifteen and lost a battle with AIDS in his early twenties.

"When my mother realized that she had three sons who were gay," Leonard says, leaning back in his chair, "gay people weren't 'stinky things' anymore. They were respectable people. It made a difference in her life."

A graduate of Morehouse College, Leonard works full-time

LEONARD GREEN (LEFT) AND STEVE LANGLEY AT THE REFLECTING POOL IN FRONT OF THE WASHINGTON MONUMENT.

"*Everyone wants, you know, to have a lovable lover. Well, we don't have that luxury. Because of my politics.*"

for the New York Health Department. But he's received most of his notoriety from his part-time work as editor and publisher of the *Right Angle*, a gay conservative newsletter.

"Leonard has a reputation," says Steve, "so when my friends found out that he's my lover, some of them wanted to break us up, wanted to know why I was involved with him. Some people felt sorry for me. I had to explain that I loved him as a person, that I certainly don't agree with him on all those issues, and he doesn't agree with everything I write and sing, but we put that aside."

"Everyone wants, you know, to have a lovable lover," Leonard says. "Well, we don't have that luxury. Because of my politics."

Leonard's politics also have affected Steve's career as a performing artist. Formerly a member of the Flirtations, the doo-wop group that appeared in the movie *Philadelphia*, Steve now appears solo around Washington, D.C., his home town, and performs with Reverb, an a-cappella group that tours the world. He's actually lost bookings at events because organizers don't want Leonard there. Sometimes, though, his appearances have been canceled for more spiteful reasons.

"They just want to punish us for being together," Steve says, shrugging his shoulders.

Steve's relationship with Leonard used to be part of the Flirtations' act. During a section of the show called "One of Us," each member would reveal a biographical fact about another member of the group—"One of us was in the Army," and so on. One of the singers would say, "One of us is in a long-term relationship with a Republican." Audiences would invariably hiss.

"Afterward, very few people would guess who it was," says Steve.

Steve never guessed that a vacation in New Orleans would end in true love. A savvy traveler, he had written ahead to what he thought was a black gay organization in the city, hoping to meet someone who could show him around. But when a Mr. Cohen from the organization contacted him to let him know that a Leonard Green would be his guide, Steve assumed it was in fact a Jewish gay group.

"I thought, 'So, now I'm gonna be shown around by a white guy. Okay. Whatever. I want to meet people," he recalls.

When Leonard came to the door, Steve spied him through the peephole.

"I said, 'Oh, he's black. A surprise!' And we've been together ever since," Steve says.

By the second day of Steve's vacation, Leonard was introducing him as his lover. "I moved quickly because I had a gut feeling that I had found the person that I needed," Leonard says. "Because, see, if you're dealing with a lot of political stuff, you want your personal life to be balanced. You want that to be taken care of. I don't want a political person as a lover."

The two men began a long-distance relationship that lasted three years, until Leonard moved to Washington, where they lived for four years. Now they live in New York City, though they still keep a house in D.C., where Steve spends most of his time.

Together, Leonard and Steve embody the romantic adage that opposites attract. And despite their differences, they are best friends.

"I think that's one of the keys that has kept us together," says Steve. "He puts my feelings first. So we're constantly trying to please each other."

"Certainly we have different views when it comes to politics, you know, and other issues too," Leonard says, "but the bottom line is that regardless of what Steve may say or what I may say— the bottom line is that we love each other."

DAVID CHANNELL AND JEROME SZYMCZAK

===

Okay, so maybe David Channell's pickup line wasn't the most provocative—"You want a peanut?" he asked Jerome Szymczak in a Milwaukee gay bar—but it worked.

"Then we went home," Jerry laughs.

"The three of us," adds David, grinning.

It was 1974. Then a nineteen-year-old student at the University of Wisconsin at Milwaukee, Jerry had been seeing an older student, Greg, a teaching assistant from one of his classes.

"He kind of seduced me," Jerry recalls, "even though I think I was an old nineteen and I was certainly ready for the experience. At the time it involved a lot of drinking and staying out all night and plopping into bed together."

It was during just such a night that Jerry ran into David, who was living in Milwaukee temporarily, trying to arrange visitation rights for his son with his estranged wife.

David invited Jerry and Greg home with him.

"I said I had some pot," David says, "and we got back there and in a few minutes we all started getting amorous toward each other. But Greg sees that he's being left out and gets upset and goes to the bathroom. I knew right away that Jerry was a good person because he took the time to slow down and go talk to Greg."

"Greg was crying," Jerry says, "and I said, 'I'm sorry. I didn't plan it this way, but I want to stay.' So I stayed, and three days later David and I got out of bed."

The next few days were a confusing time for David and Jerry. David says he was so obsessed he could hardly think straight, let alone concentrate on his work at a Milwaukee frame shop.

"I wanted this guy to be the love of my life," David says in his gentle English accent. "I was head over heels, instantly in love."

Jerry was under the impression that a one-night stand—even if it's a good one-night stand—is the only way it goes for gay men.

So when David showed up at his house a few days later, Jerry was shocked.

"I had never met a gay man who was normal," Jerry says. "This person I was involved with, this T.A., Greg, was drunk and depressed most of the time. The people I was meeting at the bars were outrageous, were drunk or hairdressers—not that there's anything wrong with hairdressers—but it was like if you're going to be queer, you're going to be a poodle cutter or a hairdresser and you're going to drink too much."

Weeks later David and Jerry found themselves walking giddily around the city together, throwing bottles stuffed with their names into a lake, doing that "whole *Love Story* thing," as David calls it.

But there were some hesitations. Their age difference may have been partly to blame. David was twenty-nine. He had been married. He had lived abroad. Jerry had never really left Milwaukee.

"I sort of felt like I had had a life and seen a lot when we met, and maybe he should do that too," David says, "and maybe the timing's off by ten years, but goddamn it I hope not."

Two months later Jerry would get his chance to see the world—or at least a lot more of the United States. He and David set off on a two-month hitchhiking tour, first to Florida to see David's son, and then to Mexico. Next they had planned to become hippies in Oregon, but when a friend offered them a place to stay rent-free in Berkeley, California, for a few months, they stopped by—and stayed for ten years. They still live nearby, on the tiny island of Alameda.

Over time Jerry gradually realized that David wasn't just a buddy he was occasionally sleeping with as he hitchhiked across the country. "I think by the time we got out to California it occurred to me that I had started a new life," Jerry says. "I thought, 'This is who I am and it's great and I love it and not only can I leave all those roots behind, I can leave that part of myself behind too.' "

They've been living with and loving each other for twenty-one years now. They own and operate a framing shop in Berkeley, but sometimes they work at home—David on his poetry and other writing projects, Jerry on his own writing projects. But during the day they mostly stay out of each other's way.

"My dining room table is my office," David says. "Jerry has another office in another room. We make each other coffee every morning, and then he's off."

Time seems to pass the couple by without their taking much notice, punctuated only by regular vacations to Europe or the Caribbean. They rarely spend time contemplating the fact that they've spent so many years together.

David says it's only in the last six months that he and Jerry have looked at each other and recognized that they're happy together and compatible and they've acknowledged their lives are good.

"I've been searching for contentment over happiness and have achieved a greater degree of happiness as a result," David says, looking intently at the man he's shared most of his life with. "Just recently I became aware that it's lasted so long, and I've begun reveling in that. I don't think we ever said to each other five or ten years ago, 'Look how happy we are.'

"We're amazed, too. It's what I wanted from the minute I offered him peanuts, of course, but I didn't know that it could happen."

*"**I**'ve been searching for contentment over happiness and have achieved a greater degree of happiness as a result. Just recently I became aware that it's lasted so long, and I've begun reveling in that. I don't think we ever said to each other five or ten years ago, 'Look how happy we are.' "*

BRENT HAWKES AND JOHN SPROULE

I t was days after the second-largest mass arrest in Canadian history—the Canadian Stonewall, if you will. In 1981, Toronto police ordered that gay bathhouses were indecent and had to be shut down. More than three hundred people were arrested in one night, and the Reverend Brent Hawkes, minister of Toronto's Metropolitan Community Church, began a hunger strike that would last twenty-five days, until the city appointed an outside investigator to look into the incident.

Every evening during the hunger strike John Sproule turned up at the church for a candlelight vigil and communion service. Afterwards he stayed to chat with Brent. A romance soon blossomed.

Brent likes to say that after twenty-five days without food, "I couldn't fight him off any longer."

But John says it was Brent who did the pursuing; John just allowed himself to be caught. "I ran slowly," he says.

The church that brought the couple together has grown and matured along with their relationship. In recent years, the congregation has swollen from fifty to five hundred and fifty. It's now the third largest MCC fellowship in the world.

"It's a Christian church with a special ministry to the gay and lesbian community," Brent says. "Our job is to reach out to gays and lesbians who have given up on the church—either because they were kicked out or bored out." It is a church founded on principles of spirituality, community, and social justice—principles that Brent and John take very seriously. Political and social demonstrations sponsored by MCC are as common as bake sales at other churches. In 1986, MCC helped pass Toronto's Bill 7, which extends the protection of the city's civil rights laws to gays and lesbians. The church also fought vigorously in support of the 1996 Canadian Human Rights Act, which included sexual orientation and passed overwhelmingly nationwide. And MCC hosts huge services every year for the approximately 750,000 participants in Toronto's Pride Day festivities.

BRENT HAWKES (LEFT) AND JOHN SPROULE IN TORONTO'S METROPOLITAN COMMUNITY CHURCH.

"*K*eeping the house going and being there for him—it's part of being a minister's spouse, and that in itself is a taxing lot, and most minister's spouses out there would relate to the same sort of thing. It's part of the deal."

"We're not going to be a closeted church," Brent promises. Raised as a strict Baptist, Brent began to feel he was called to the ministry in junior high. But later, when he realized he was gay, he decided he couldn't go to divinity school. Instead, he became a high-school teacher. "I felt like I was abandoning my best friend—God," he says.

Then, one day in the mid-1970s, Brent picked up a copy of the *Advocate* and spotted an ad for the MCC fellowship. "I cried," he says, "because I knew this is where I belonged."

He moved to Toronto in 1976 and became a pastor at the church the following year. Now, nineteen years later, he's working on his divinity doctoral degree.

Not surprisingly, Brent's work doesn't make everyone in Canada happy. Two years ago, after MCC's very public stand on same-sex spousal benefits and recognition, Brent began receiving death threats.

"Police insisted that I wear a bulletproof vest and they provided bodyguards during the worship service for Pride Day," he says.

It doesn't make loving him easy.

"It goes with the territory," says John with a sigh. "Nobody likes that kind of death-threat thing. I guess I look at it as Brent has many unique skills that I can enable. And keeping the house going and being there for him—it's part of being a minister's spouse, and that in itself is a taxing lot, and most minister's spouses out there would relate to the same sort of thing. It's part of the deal."

"Life hasn't been easy at times," Brent agrees. "I have no illusion at all that without John, I wouldn't be able to last nineteen years and do what I do."

Today, Brent and John share a 100-year-old house with twelve-foot cathedral ceilings, three fireplaces, two dogs (Munchkin and J. J.), and a garden out back. But during their first few years as a couple they kept separate apartments even though they spent every night together. When they did start sharing a place, John refused to give up his set of dishes or silverware or toaster—for years.

"It was certainly my initiative that kept the relationship going for those years," says Brent. "I found John very sincere and honest, and he was a good pastor's spouse, and he was respectable. . . . It felt right."

"It took me awhile to figure out if this is where I wanted to be," John explains. "You're not thinking about a few years away. You're sort of thinking, 'Where do you want to go to dinner tonight?' "

John did eventually start thinking long-term, says Brent: "While we were walking in Key West on vacation a long time ago, John said to me, 'You know, this would be a great city for us to retire in.' And I said, 'It sounds like you want to be in a relationship.' 'Oh, shut up,' he said. That's when I knew."

But it took fifteen years for Brent to get John to the altar. After the first few years of unsuccessful attempts, he stopped trying and asked John to come to holy union classes when he was ready.

"One night we were in just sort of a romantic mood coming home from visiting my parents and I said okay," John recalls. "Going through a holy union is a real commitment—not to be done lightly."

"You waited fifteen years," Brent says. "Sometimes John is a bit provincial."

"One wants to be sure," John says.

"John's mom is a devout Catholic so she was quite pleased when John finally decided to settle down and bring a priest home," cracks Brent.

JOHN LILLEY AND BOB LOHRMANN

John Lilley is trying to get Bob Lohrmann to tell one of his stories.

Bob's got a million of them. It's one of the things John loves most about him after seventeen years together—his stories and his face when it's screwed up in laughter.

"That's the face I love," John says, after an outburst of Bob's hearty chuckle.

Bob tells a story from the early days of their relationship. They weren't living together yet; Bob was still living in an apartment that also housed the theater company he worked for in Malvern, Pennsylvania. His friend, Doug, called him a few months after he started seeing John to get an update on their relationship.

"I said, 'He's really pushing it. Really fast. I'm just not sure.'

"Doug said, 'What do you mean?' "

A few nights before, John had shown up really late at Bob's apartment—completely unexpected. Bob heard him open the door and clunk up the stairs with his guitar slung over his shoulder.

"He didn't even call me," Bob remembers telling Doug. He says it now with mock irritation. "He just took his guitar off, stripped off all his clothes, and climbed into bed with me."

There was silence for a second on the other line, then Doug replied, "Are you out of your mind? You're complaining about this?"

"And I said, 'I guess you're right,' " Bob says, laughing again. He had nothing to complain about.

John Lilley joined a neighborhood band in the 1970s and got lucky. By the mid-1980s the Hooters had scored a handful of hits ("And We Danced," "All You Zombies," "Day By Day"), and John was suddenly propelled into a rock & roll world of fame, wealth, and crazed groupies. He and Bob had been together about four years when the Hooters landed in the spotlight; the couple was unprepared for all the attention and its consequences.

"It was strange getting used to the financial adjustment and to

JOHN LILLEY (RIGHT) AND BOB LOHRMANN AT THEIR VACATION HOME ON VIEQUES, OFF PUERTO RICO'S EAST COAST.

"*W*hat's mine is yours and what's yours is mine'—that's the way I wanted it to be. A pretty easy decision to make when I was the one making significantly less money. But the fact was that it was a barrier. Money is power in a relationship.*"

people recognizing you all the time," says John, who was not out of the closet then. "People would drive by our house at three in the morning playing our songs, you know? Girls would come by and look in the window and see me vacuuming, like, in my underwear. It freaked us both out. It's hard to live that way."

Bob and John eventually got used to the road trips, the celebrity, the videos on MTV, playing huge concerts like Live Aid, and the glamour of it all—but not before it wreaked some serious havoc on their relationship.

"It was probably the hardest period of time in our lives," Bob says. "It was hard because of the different levels our careers were at. John was having trouble dealing with the success and all that. I was having trouble dealing with his success. 'What's mine is yours and what's yours is mine'—that's the way I wanted it to be. A pretty easy decision to make when I was the one making significantly less money. But the fact was that it was a barrier. Money is power in a relationship."

"Finally," John says, "I said 'We're sharing.' Why was this even an issue at all?"

Therapy helped, but so did the history of their relationship. John met Bob at a straight rock & roll bar. At the time Bob had been married for two years but was trying "an open relationship that included men" with his wife.

John had more serious intentions. "I was looking for stability in my life," he says. "I was looking for a real relationship. I wanted someone who wouldn't drive me crazy. I was looking for a real man."

But Bob was too confused to make an immediate move. He kept John at a bay for months, until he could discuss the future of his marriage with his wife over Christmas.

John says the waiting made for a stressful holiday, but he didn't give up. "Finally Bob called and said we were going to happen," he remembers, smiling, "and I felt so relieved and so happy."

Today John is still happy. Although the Hooters are no longer so much in the spotlight as they once were, John now produces music bits for radio stations nationwide and still travels with the band a few times a year on tours through Europe, where they have a dedicated following.

Bob's career, too, has become successful. For the past ten years he's directed the audience-driven play *Shear Madness* at the Kennedy Center in Washington, D.C. Ticket sales are anything but dwindling—it's the longest-running non-musical show in the history of American theater.

Their careers having balanced out with time, Bob and John now live a relatively quiet, nested life in West Chester, Pennsylvania. They take pleasure in an occasional getaway to their second home in Puerto Rico, where they say they might retire someday. But at forty-two and forty-four respectively, John and Bob are in no hurry. They're content to follow their careers wherever they lead, to pursue other interests as they see fit, and to spend quiet evenings enjoying each other's company.

"I'm planning things in my life other than rock & roll," says John, who has taken up gardening as something more than a pastime. He's started a landscaping company and wants to go back to school to study horticulture. "I'm not going to play rock & roll the rest of my life."

"It's hard to be a screaming rocker when you're sixty-five," agrees Bob, teasing his partner lovingly. "Nowadays we're so happy to rent a movie and sit at home and watch a foreign film or something. It's rather normal, not what you'd expect in your fantasies about the rock & roll experience."

DEAN T. HARA AND GERRY STUDDS

In 1983, after ten years as a U.S. Representative for the state of Massachusetts, Gerry Studds was dragged kicking and screaming from the closet when a relationship he had with a male Capitol Hill page was revealed.

"It was," he says, "a serious error in judgment."

On the floor of Congress he acknowledged his homosexuality publicly, saying, "My sexual preference has nothing to do with my ability to do this job well or to do it badly."

He never apologized.

"I was goddamned if I was going to be the most recent in a series of countries with gay people who said, 'Excuse me, sorry. I'll go away.' I told them to stuff it," says Gerry. "It was none of their business."

Gerry considered every option and then chose to run for re-election after the scandal broke. He decided that running again—not running away—was the right thing to do. He didn't expect to win, but he did—and he would do so again and again,

returning to his congressional post for another five terms.

"The fact that we could somehow shake that disaster," he says on the eve of his retirement from twenty-four years in office, "and make a triumph out of it in the long term was something that I never thought possible."

Dean Hara remembers reading about Gerry's troubles in the newspaper and watching the reports on television.

"I wanted to send a note or get in contact with him, but I didn't," he says. "I probably felt at that point that he wouldn't even remember me, and it wouldn't make any difference."

Dean had met Gerry four years earlier in a bar. Dean was twenty-one and had just moved to Washington, D.C. Gerry was a fourth-term, closeted congressman who was just beginning—occasionally—to go out to gay bars and meet people. Dean says that at the time he had no idea who Gerry was.

"I was trying to get him to talk and he would not do it," Dean

recalls. "I asked him, 'Where did you grow up?' And then, 'What did you do?' and so on until I got to 1970, when he said, 'I ran for Congress.'

"And then he said that he lost. I kept prodding, and he said, 'Well, I ran for Congress again in 1972.' I asked, 'And *then* what happened?' And he said, 'I won.' And I'm like, 'Oh my God.' "

After a few dates Dean and Gerry stopped seeing each other for the next twelve years—not necessarily because they wanted to.

"I put him away to age for a decade," Gerry jokes. "I couldn't get my own act together. We're almost twenty years apart—twenty years and two weeks to the day. He was gorgeous. He was too young. I was too un-me. I was in the beginning process of coming out to myself and my friends, never mind to the world. I just had no experience. I didn't have my teenage years and my twenties to experiment like everybody is supposed to have. I didn't know what I was doing."

Dean and Gerry would run into each other every couple of years—Dean never forgot the phone number to Gerry's office— but nothing developed until they bumped into each other on Du Pont Circle, at J. R.'s, in 1991.

By then, Dean had sown most of his oats in the District. And at age fifty, Gerry was now more experienced, having been through two long-term relationships, both of which ended badly. Dean had also matured.

"When we met I was twenty-one, and not only was I dealing with a member of Congress . . ." says Dean, who has just begun graying at the temples, "I think the twenty-year age difference makes a much bigger difference when you're in your early twenties than when you're in your early thirties."

Later that year Gerry proposed, and in January 1997 the couple celebrated their six-year anniversary. Over the course of those years, Dean has learned that being committed to Gerry also means being committed to his political career.

"It's more of a burden than on the average spouse," says Gerry.

Dean tows the party line with anyone he meets. He is Gerry's biggest supporter.

"Gays in the military?" he says. "It started here in this office. Gerry, I think, has probably moved the gay community further [than other leaders] and has never really gotten the credit that he deserves."

He is also Gerry's closest advisor. When the Massachusetts state legislature mandated a restructuring of Gerry's district in 1992, Gerry lost a third of his most ardent voters and considered not running for re-election.

"We walked around the Capitol that night," Dean recalls, "and I said, 'If you give up now, everybody's going to say that they've won—they got you out of office. If you run, if you win, you have the possibility of proving them all wrong and serving under a Democratic president for the first time in twelve years."

Dean's role as a political spouse also means being at Gerry's side for official events.

"It's intimidating," Dean says. "It's one thing to have dinner with a small group of friends. It's another to go to the White House as an openly gay couple. It surprises me when Teddy Kennedy comes over and says, 'Hi Dean. How are you?' I'm just kind of tongue-tied. It doesn't seem real."

"It's quite wonderful really," says Gerry. "I've often said, especially to gay audiences, that I think the most important things we do are ironically the most routine. It's not so much the grand speeches . . . "Those who know of our commitment range from our closest friends and family to the President and Vice-President of the United States, who know Dean by name. It's astonishing."

He's right about the power of small victories. There's something incredibly heartening, something triumphant about an engraved invitation from the White House addressed to "Congressman Gerry Studds and Mr. Dean Hara."

But after twenty-four years of such victories, Gerry has decided to chart a new course in his life—one that leads out of politics. Tired of the campaigning, the seediness of 1990s politics, and never being able to make dinner plans because the House is so unpredictable, he's ready to move back to Cape Cod, where he built a home in 1983.

"My heart and soul and mortgage have always been in Provincetown," he says.

Dean is giving up his appointed post in public relations for the Department of the Interior and will focus instead on the interior of the couple's newly purchased Boston brownstone.

It's a dream come true for Gerry. "I have wanted more than anything else to have a home of my own, a person to share it with, and a nest that is truly ours—not your parents, not some rental that's just part of your job," he says. "Crate & Barrel is a pretty exciting place to go."

LOUIS CERUZZI AND BOB PILLA

Atlanta is about twenty percent gay. But don't tell the locals. "It's a southern thing," says Louis Ceruzzi, a North Carolina native who once moved to New York to work for Macy's, then transferred back to Dixie because he missed home. "Gay people move here from all of these very oppressive southern cities. They can move to this big city where there is an acceptance. It's a white collar, liberal town and they can still get their collards and black-eyed peas."

Bob Pilla, Louis's lover of ten years, relocated from Philadelphia to Atlanta six months after meeting Louis. "Atlanta has this reputation," Bob says. "It's the birthplace of Martin Luther King. It's a place where minorities can feel that they are a part of things—that they can feel comfortable."

Pay attention during the city's morning rush hour and you'll see pairs of neatly dressed men in Jeeps and Lexuses and BMWs and Saturns heading to work together. Nothing particularly unusual about that except for the great ties they wear and, of course, the telltale rainbow sticker. Some Atlantans may not notice it, but this symbol of gay pride can be spotted on flags, decals, and bumper stickers as often as the more controversial and almost as pervasive "Stars and Bars"—the confederate battle flag that is still a widely revered symbol of the Old South.

Old South or no, one of the top-five largest gay populations in the country has to shop, and that's where Bob and Louis come in. Together they own Wish, a bright, hipster boutique in Little Five Points, Atlanta's trendiest, most youthful borough. They also own Curve, Wish's gay little brother, across town in Ansley Mall.

"I wish there was no need for this store," says Louis of Curve in his thick, southern drawl. "I wish I could get everyone to go to Five Points, but not everyone feels comfortable there." He is referring to Wish, the larger, straight-friendly store that attracts the pseudo-punks, skateboarders, and rave kids of the borough.

"In the future a gay store will be unnecessary," Louis continues, still thinking aloud. "For now, though, in Atlanta, it makes sense."

LOUIS CERUZZI (LEFT) AND BOB PILLA IN THE BACKYARD OF THEIR ATLANTA HOME.

Curve was originally named Physikos when Louis opened it four years ago. It's tucked away in the Ansley Mall, a shopping plaza in the heart of Atlanta's gayest district. Blocks away is the mostly gay apartment complex Ansley Forest. Throw a brick and you'll hit a gay bar. Throw another in the summer and you'll hit a muscled young man that humidity has drawn out of his tank top.

Louis closed Physikos and left Ansley when kilts and hot pants went out of vogue with the gym crowd. "They got into such good shape that they didn't want to wear shirts anymore," he says. But he and Bob have just re-opened the boutique—as Curve—as part of their vision for a gay-owned national clothing chain.

It's a vision that has grown out of their common experiences as they built their relationship and, later, their business, all the while trying to maintain their own sense of identity in the face of convenient labels and categories used to define them by gays and straights alike.

In January of 1986, Louis went to see a psychic. He was thirty, single, living in New York, and desperate. He wanted a relationship.

"I said, 'I gotta find out if I am ever going to meet someone,'" he recalls. "It was time."

The psychic told him he would meet someone significant soon—someone younger, in another city. Three months later, bored with New York's nightlife, Louis went with a friend to Philadelphia. That's where he met Bob—a younger man.

"It was like this big *ka-chang*!" says Louis. "I knew that night. He was the person I was looking for."

Bob was twenty-three then and hadn't been thinking seriously about a relationship. He was more concerned about figuring out life on his own. The next afternoon he had plans to move into downtown Philadelphia, out of his parents' house in the suburbs.

"Louis was a nice guy. I liked him," says Bob, "but I figured he'd go back to New York and that would be pretty much it."

"I had to court him," says Louis, grinning.

"Louis kind of thought that I was going to move to New York but I'm not really fond of New York."

Fortunately neither was Louis. When Macy's offered him a job in Atlanta as a vice-president of merchandising, he accepted. "It was a gamble," he says today, "but I had gotten tired of New York. Everyone was getting sick, and I guess I thought I could run away."

Ultimately Bob needed to run away too. Moving out of his family's home hadn't made life any easier. He had dropped out of college, and Louis was impatiently waiting in Atlanta. "It was a good move," Bob says. "Being far away from my family—we could have a better relationship here. It's easier for me being down here to live the way I want and not have to worry about them."

For seven years or so, Bob and Louis enjoyed a relatively quiet, anonymous life as a gay couple in a mostly straight condo complex. With the help and support of Louis, Bob finished college at Georgia State and went to work at Macy's. But Louis was getting antsy. He wanted his own retail store, so he opened Physikos in 1993. As the owner of a hot new store, he went from being an unknown guy with a buzz cut to a local gay celebrity. And Bob became known as "the lover of the owner of Physikos."

The space between the two, which Bob says was vital to making their relationship work, evaporated when they decided to share not only their lives but also their work by opening Wish in 1994. They shared the same tiny office for months. It nearly destroyed their relationship. But Bob wasn't going to let that happen.

"I would go floating into the damn stratosphere if it weren't for Bob," Louis says. "Bob pulls me down and brings me back to earth and Bob also keeps me from working all the time. I couldn't have achieved any of this [alone]. We've always been independent. We've always had separation, and that was too close. The business has been a difficult thing for us to go through and a real strain on our relationship, and I think if we hadn't had all those years of foundation going into it . . ."

They're still here, though, still together, and ready to try a second store again—"because of what we have," says Bob. "We're together for life and we love each other. He knew right away. It took me awhile but I know now, too. Some people believe in a soul mate . . . I do, and we were definitely meant to be together. We can handle it." Still, he says, "I often wish that these stores didn't exist, sometimes."

"It was so nice before when I had this big, high-paying job at Macy's," says Louis. "I only worked forty hours a week and I got off early on Fridays. I had the whole weekend free. We had really nice vacations. We had Friday night together. We had all day Saturday. Now we barely have Sunday. It's been a real intrusion on our relationship. Now obviously, if it works out as it gets bigger it will all be worth it. And it looks like it might be."

They won't be getting married to celebrate.

"We are not heterosexuals and we don't wish to indulge in the rituals that they do," says Bob diplomatically.

Louis is more emphatic. "We don't need it," he shouts, his eyebrows arching into perfect right angles. "We have our own relationship that we've created and it doesn't fall into a neat category. . . . We don't understand why gay people feel like they have to have the trappings of heterosexual commitment in order to have a valid relationship. God save us from straight-acting. We're two men."

"Everyone wants to look 'normal,' " Bob says. "Needless to say, Louis is fighting that tooth and nail."

Every once in a while the light catches the silver of the nipple rings on Louis's chest. They gleam through his vintage mesh football jersey. He also wears a large single hoop through his left ear—not just hanging from the earlobe, mind you, but *through* the midsection of his ear. His hair is cut into a buzzed, spiked mohawk, and his blue cords and neon-green sneakers are right on time.

"Gay people are taken aback by his look," says Bob, who has his own style, as well. He looks like a teenage military cadet in his Firestone T-shirt, cut-off jeans, and Adidas trainers.

Louis smiles and says, "Gay people in many ways are naturally creative and artistic. And back in the day, I mean, *back in the day*, we were on the edge and expressive and ahead of the trends. No one ever told me that those days are over."

Louis's natural tendency to be an outcast led him to open Physikos in the first place. After Federated Department Stores took over Macy's he knew he'd have to move on. He didn't look conservative enough for the new bosses. And although management told him they were okay with his homosexuality he sensed that wasn't true. "Macy's just squashed and repressed me," Louis says. "It's as much a grudge match as anything to show what a gay person can do outside of a corporation."

"It's a positive thing for the gay community," Bob says.

"The store is something we can look to and say it's a successful business run by gay people for gay people," says Louis. "People need to see that we can do it. My goal is to create a very large and powerful corporation based in this city that will be a model for diversity and acceptance and a real economic force that can be a proponent for change on a regional level and maybe one day national."

Then, adds Louis with a crooked grin, "Why shouldn't there be a gay Ted Turner?"

DAN BUTLER AND RICHARD WATERHOUSE

There is an unwritten rule in Hollywood that most actors—male and female, gay and straight—tend to follow religiously: Never date another actor. Four years ago, working actors Dan Butler and Richard Waterhouse ignored that rule.

"I used to think that actors shouldn't date actors," says Richard in the makeshift kitchen of his and Dan's new Los Angeles home. "Now I can't imagine it another way."

Dan and Richard discovered each other—not surprisingly in Los Angeles—on the stage. In 1990, years before they started dating, Richard and his partner at the time, Philip, went to see Terrance McNally's *Lisbon Traviata*, in which Dan had the starring role.

"In it," Richard recalls, "Dan walks out on stage in a towel, having just come out of the shower, and he looked really beautiful. He looked great in a towel, and the whole audience, a lot of gay men . . . you could just hear the guys going 'Ummmmmm. Who's that?' And I thought, 'God, he's really sexy.' "

Dan spotted Richard three years later in a benefit performance of *Oliver Twisted*, part of Los Angeles's Charity Parodies, a series that tweaks well-known stage shows with a gay sensibility.

"I was pretty smitten," says Dan, who is best known as the outrageously heterosexual Bob "Bulldog" Brisco on NBC's *Frasier*. "I asked about him the next day and found out that he was with a lover of five years [Philip], and unfortunately . . . well, a lot of things were happening in my life, too."

When Philip died from AIDS-related illness in 1994, Dan was in rehearsal for his acclaimed one-man stage show, *The Only Thing Worse You Could Have Told Me*, with his director Randy Brenner—who happened to be a mutual friend of Dan and Richard's.

"So, he's available," is the first thing Dan remembers saying after hearing about Philip's death. "And Randy says, 'Dan!' And so the whole day I felt like this schmuck. And I said, '*Please* tell him I'm sorry.' "

Richard suspected that Dan was the right guy, but he felt guilty

DAN BUTLER (RIGHT) AND RICHARD WATERHOUSE IN THE BACKYARD OF THEIR HOLLYWOOD HILLS HOME.

for thinking this only four months after losing Philip.

"I didn't know when to take off the black dress," Richard says, stirring a bowl of homemade chicken soup. "I told Randy I felt like Scarlett O'Hara in a red dress, dancing. 'You know,' I said. 'I shouldn't be dancing right now.' "

Dan didn't want to force things either. "I sort of spoke to Philip," he says. "Just saying, 'I'm not trying to encroach on your territory or anything.' Because it felt weird. I went to the cabin that they had built in Arizona and I was staying overnight at the house that was Philip's that Richard had moved into. I was sort of making peace with spirits or whatever."

"I remember coming home from a date [with Dan] and saying to my friend Andy, 'This could be something really big if he could slow down,' " says Richard, rubbing Dan's stomach. "Because it was sooooo soon for me. I needed to take it kind of slower. I knew that this could be a real biggie. And you don't expect a biggie right after a biggie. You expect a series of toads."

Dan did slow down, and he and Richard have been together ever since. They still seem to be on their honeymoon, though.

Together they bought this quaint English Tudor house in the hills of Los Angeles that looks like something from a Brothers Grimm tale. It will require months of work for them to personal-

ize it. Already Richard has helped sheet-rock the entryway, and Dan has ripped down the dry wall from their future kitchen.

"You know," Dan says, "when we first came in here, the sun room sort of sloped a little, and we were concerned. And then we found out that engineering-wise it's fine. It's a seventy-year-old house that's on a slope. It will never be perfect, and I think that's a good analogy for a relationship."

"There's a charming imperfection of it," Richard agrees. "There's a lot of charm of us."

As they share chicken soup and oatmeal-raisin cookies on their unfinished first floor, Dan and Richard are comfortably affectionate with one another. They talk about their still-young relationship and study each other's faces.

"I think the really great thing about a relationship or a long-term relationship is when you fall in love with one another all over again," Dan says. "I think that's the biggest, *biggest* perk to being in a long-term relationship. It's like a season. You can count on it coming back. I was in a seven-year relationship, and this seems twice as long as that. It just seems like we've already been together awhile."

Richard nods in agreement. "I don't have any plans to go anywhere else," he says. "This is where I want to be."

TOM CIANO AND TOM MORGAN

_T_heir eyes met across a crowded room.

It was 1982, in Washington, D.C., at the Palm restaurant. Tom Ciano and Tom Morgan were lunching on business—at separate tables —and neither one spoke to the other. They just stared. And stared.

"You just know," says Morgan. "I thought if he wasn't gay, he was at least interested."

"I didn't think you were straight," Ciano says, smiling broadly.

Ciano and Morgan sit in the living room of the Brooklyn brownstone they've shared for the past nine years. Throughout the house—on the dining room table, in the kitchen, on side tables in this room—are handmade ceramic artifacts, evidence of one of Morgan's hobbies since he left his job at the _New York Times_ on permanent disability in 1994.

Morgan has AIDS. Ciano is HIV-negative but he, too, has made adjustments to his professional life. He continues to work as a consultant in low-income housing development but organizes his schedule to have as much time as possible to spend with Tom in their sprawling garden out back or refurbishing the home that will be a legacy of their twelve-year partnership.

It's a partnership that didn't take root until about two years after lunch at the Palm. A few months after that first encounter, Ciano and Morgan ran into each other at the YMCA.

"I thought he was gay in the restaurant, but when I saw him at the gym I assumed he was straight," Ciano says.

Morgan thought Ciano had a girlfriend. "We were both working out, but he had come with his sister . . . I didn't know she was his sister. I remember saying to someone, 'Damn. He's straight.' "

A conversation in the gym led to lunch, but Morgan's nervousness prevented him from eating.

"My reaction was to eat my lunch and then finish his," Ciano says.

A relationship was brewing, but there were complications. Morgan was dating someone else. Ciano's life was in transition—

TOM CIANO (LEFT) AND TOM MORGAN IN THE LIVING ROOM OF THEIR BROOKLYN BROWNSTONE.

he was coming to terms with being openly gay, ending a long-term relationship with another man, and leaving Washington for graduate school at Columbia University. He moved to New York three months later.

"I remember having a very deep feeling for Tom but knowing that I couldn't put my energies into it because I was moving and he was with someone and I had done that long-distance thing and I couldn't do it again."

"I knew that I wanted him," Morgan says. But ask him why in 1984 he left his job at the *Washington Post* for another at the *New York Times*, and he'll say it wasn't for Ciano. "I knew I would see him, but I wasn't making any effort," he says.

For his part, Ciano was in therapy—"to find out why I was doing certain things"—and dealing with his intense graduate program. He was pretty sure that Morgan was Mr. Right, but he wanted to explore his freedom and think carefully before making any commitments.

"It wasn't just, 'Oh, I met this gorgeous man I'm in love with,'" Ciano recalls. "It was much more, 'I think this is someone I can work on a relationship with.' For me, I had evolved where I needed to [be independent] before I could be in a relationship, so it doesn't mean that I loved Tom any less. It just meant I needed to work on some things."

"It was rocky for the first year or so," Morgan says.

"I wouldn't say rocky," Ciano gently counters. "We had defined it as 'We're free to date other people,' and I was too busy to, honestly—I just didn't."

Except once. A gym instructor asked him out to dinner. They ended up at Ernie's, a cavernous restaurant on the west side.

"There were hundreds of people there, or so it seemed. And who is two tables away from me?" Ciano asks. "So this guy's all in my face: 'How come you're not in a relationship?' I said, 'I am in a relationship—with this guy two tables over.'"

Two tables away Morgan was dining with an HBO vice-president who was grilling him with some of the same questions. "It was really very funny because after Tom stopped by the table to say good-bye, [my date] asked me who he was. 'Well,' I said. 'That's the guy I'm dating.' And I never saw [my date] again."

"I think we both realized at that point that we had dated other people enough. It's one of those life-changing moments . . ." Ciano laughs, grabbing Morgan's knee, "at Ernie's."

After Ciano finished grad school he and Morgan moved to Brooklyn together.

"It was less important to be in the middle of everything in Manhattan and was more important to have a garden, a house, to have this other life," Morgan says. "We're really very active in the neighborhood. We have dinner with neighbors who are straight, and it really feels like a home."

But living together, in the same home, as a couple, meant learning new lessons. Their first rental house had terrible wallpaper, and Ciano was determined to strip it off and repaint in a new color. But he and Morgan couldn't agree on what color it should be. Ciano was so frustrated he took it to his therapist. "I remember going to therapy and saying, 'You know, here I've spent all this time stripping out wallpaper and I'm going to end up with a color I hate. It just doesn't seem right.'"

One night, in tears, he told Morgan: "I don't know if we've made the right decision. I don't want everything to be halfway between what I want and what you want and neither of us gets what we want. I'll let you make this decision; I'll make another one."

So they learned about compromise. "I think that was a good

lesson to learn early on," Ciano says. "While we do share a lot of the same interests or values, we're very different. It's not been easy always letting each other agree to be different and letting it be okay."

"I grew up with a strong awareness of how it was to be different, how it was to be black in a mostly white environment," says Morgan, who in 1956 was one of only two blacks in his elementary school.

He didn't really have friends until high school, where he made enough to become student council president. "People didn't think that a high school that was majority white would elect someone black to be its president," Morgan says, "so that was a big deal."

It wouldn't be the last time Morgan was seen as a pioneer. In 1989, he ran for another presidential office—this time to lead the 2,400-member National Association of Black Journalists. His opponents used his sexuality to campaign against him.

"I must say to the credit of the organization, people rallied to my defense," Morgan says. "I'd get phone calls from people who were friends who had let their memberships lapse. They'd say, 'I'm going to sign up just to vote for you.' "

It was an ugly, grueling election, but Morgan won in a landslide. The night he won, Ciano performed a Marilyn Monroe-esque rendition of "Happy Birthday, Mr. President . . ." in Morgan's room.

Ciano is still a little miffed that he didn't get a gift from NABJ as other First Ladies had. But, he says, "I got what I needed. I was acknowledged later in his farewell speech. I didn't feel like we were in the closet or had to pretend."

Morgan did keep one secret from NABJ—by the time he ran for president, he knew he was HIV-positive.

"My thinking was, 'I have desires, I'm not sick, and I want to do something for the association while I still can,' " Morgan says. A member of Gay Men's Health Crisis, he was all too familiar with the devastation associated with AIDS—he lost his first lover to the disease.

HIV became full-blown AIDS in early 1994, but Morgan continued working.

"I was having trouble dealing with the issue of being on disability," he says, "and what that would mean for me and how I would use my time. I made a pact with myself that as long as I could get out of the house I would—every day." That July he left his job and took up volunteer work and pottery.

Morgan's illness has been particularly difficult for Ciano, who lost his mother to a long battle with cancer. Ciano says they've stopped putting things off and found the time for everything they've wanted to do in life. Morgan is refinishing the hardwood floors upstairs. An interior decorator has been hired to organize the couple's closets. Last summer they rented a house on Fire Island even though they couldn't necessarily afford it.

"We used to see an old couple on the street and we would joke," Ciano says. "One was in a walker or on a respirator, and we'd say that was Tom because he has asthma and I was going to be the one who would have the colostomy, you know?

"I feel the loss of a future, of longevity. There were moments when I really felt like just coming home to him was a gift."

Morgan rubs his partner's neck in long, gentle strokes. "I wanted to be able to grow old together. And we know that won't happen."

BILL BUMP AND JESSE M. JAMES

Bill Bump and Jesse James have a great scheme going.

They're planning their commitment ceremony for their seventh anniversary and are in need of financing. They've told their respective families that the ceremony will be held in Jesse's hometown of Oneida, New York, but they're accepting bids to change the location.

"We're going to put it in the paper and everything," says Bill mischievously, in a threat designed to get the attention of Jesse's older brother, Pat.

"He's very homophobic—very homophobic. He just doesn't understand," Jesse says of Pat. "He doesn't want to deal with it."

Were Bill and Jesse to place a wedding announcement in Oneida's local paper, Pat's name would certainly appear as well, so he's offering thirty thousand dollars for the couple to get hitched *anywhere* but Oneida. Bill's dad, on the other hand, is decidedly more open. He has offered ten thousand dollars for the couple to host the affair in Rochester, closer to Bill's family. The ceremony will be held in Rochester, but don't tell Jesse's family.

"We have *carte blanche*," Bill says. "We don't have to follow any traditions—we can do what we want."

"A commitment ceremony is important to me because when I realized I was gay I thought I'd never be able to get married," says Jesse.

That's the way he used to think—but this is the 1990s. "Family celebrations are very important to me," he continues, explaining his desire to include family and friends in the ceremony.

"Call it a celebration of our love," says Bill.

It's a celebration that began in 1995 at Bill's birthday party. Near the end of the night, Jesse presented Bill with the ring Bill wears on his left hand today, then got down on one knee and proposed.

"Isn't that romantic?" Jesse muses. "I did it in front of a large group so he would have to say yes."

Getting their friends to accept the idea of their union was the

BILL BUMP (RIGHT) AND JESSE M. JAMES IN A PARK NEAR THEIR ROCHESTER HOME.

easy part—Bill and Jesse have even received engagement cards from friends who missed the party. It's been harder to get their families to adjust to the idea.

"My mom was like, 'Why are you doing this?'" Jesse recalls. "I'm from an awfully small town. What she knows about gays and lesbians comes from *Geraldo*—those trash talk show programs. She's slowly coming out."

Other family members are wasting no time. At a recent family picnic, one of Jesse's young nephews approached the couple and said, "My cousin is telling lies about you."

"What's she saying?" Jesse asked.

"She told me that you and Uncle Bill are gay and you're getting married," the nephew replied loudly.

Jesse's mother, within earshot, began choking on her food.

"It was hysterical," Jesse says, laughing. "I said, 'Yes Ryan, that's true.' He said, 'Cool,' and ran off to tell his cousins."

Bill told his divorced parents separately. He informed his mother of the wedding plans the day after Jesse proposed, but he waited three months to tell his father.

"I wasn't sure how he'd react toward this," Bill says. "But he's known Jesse for five years. He loves Jesse, so it wasn't as hard as I thought."

Jesse's father felt the same way about Bill and probably would have attended the ceremony, but he died in 1996.

"Growing up, Archie Bunker was nice compared to my dad,"
Jesse says, explaining that when he came out to his family, his mother hid the news from his father for months, fearing it would kill him. "But he did find out and was hurt that I hadn't told him, and we talked about it."

An avid sports fan, Jesse's father died of a heart attack watching a Pacers game, but not before having a long private talk with Bill.

"He still won't tell me what they talked about," Jesse says, leaning into his partner. "One of the saddest things is that my dad and your dad didn't get to meet each other."

Their mothers have met, though, and when the two women get together for a weekend every once in a while, it's a bonding experience like no other. Both are chain smokers who fill the house with smoke as quickly as they empty it of tons of coffee.

"Our families are very similar," says Jesse. "It's scary."

The two women have a lot to talk about. While Bill's mom joined PFLAG and began her own research on what it means to be gay, Jesse's mom still longs for a more traditional marriage.

"She always thought I would grow up, marry, produce grandchildren—things like that," Jesse says. "It bothers her because it's safe to say that I'm her favorite son and whoever I was going to marry, she knew she'd have a daughter-in-law that she really truly liked. And she does. Mom loves the hell out of Bill. She calls him her daughter-in-law."

Correction: "I'm her *favorite* daughter-in-law," says Bill.

"*We have carte blanche. We don't have to follow any traditions—we can do what we want.*"

ANDY BELL AND PAUL HICKEY

I could die tomorrow and feel really happy that I got to experience Andy and true love, real love, and a loving relationship," says Paul Hickey as he and Andy Bell settle in over champagne and cigarettes to talk about their twelve-year relationship.

Andy and Paul have just returned from Spain where they've purchased a house next door to Annie Lennox, which explains why their London home is littered with pieces of furniture and art that are wrapped and packed, ready for the move. Sting and Boy George don't live far from this roomy, modern mini-mansion in the Highgate section of London.

His reflection gleaming in the shiny surface of his grand piano, Paul tells the story of how he met Andy the year before Andy met with fame. Paul, who's thirteen years older than Andy, had been single for two years and had decided it was time to get back into the dating game—mostly because as he approached the age of forty he was frightened that he would end up spending the rest of his life alone.

"I thought if I waited any longer," he says, "I'd be too old to get another relationship."

A few years earlier he had quit his job and left his home in Carmel, California, for England, in search of a new life. One Sunday afternoon he found himself in a pub for what we in the States would call a Sunday tea dance.

"I used to live right down the street from the pub," Paul says. "It was sort of the social thing to do. You'd grab your friends and meet."

Andy, who was dating two other men at the time, also was at the pub that afternoon. Paul noticed him as soon as he walked in.

"I went, 'Woo!' " Paul says. "He looked like Sting—a young Sting with the pure white hair."

Neither spoke to the other for about two hours, until finally Andy approached Paul and tapped him on the shoulder.

"He said, 'Excuse me, would you mind if we saw each other sometime?' You know, real English and polite," Paul recalls. "I

ANDY BELL (BELOW) AND PAUL HICKEY IN THE GARDEN OF HIGHSTONE HOUSE, THEIR LONDON HOME.

“*He said, 'Excuse me, would you mind if we saw each other sometime?' You know, real English and polite.*

I said, 'Honey, you could spend any time you want with me. How about right now?' From that moment on I didn't let him go.”

said, 'Honey, you could spend any time you want with me. How about right now?' From that moment on I didn't let him go."

A year later, in 1986, Andy became the voice of the pop duo Erasure, one of the world's most successful and longest-lasting bands. Since the beginning, most of Erasure's core audience has been gay and lesbian. Perhaps we're attracted to Andy's angelic falsetto; perhaps it's the lovesick angst he wrings from hits such as "Sometimes," "Chains of Love," "A Little Respect," and "Oh l'Amour;" or maybe it's just because of Erasure's infinitely danceable beat.

Back then, Andy's decision to have an openly gay persona and songwriting sensibility was against Paul's wishes. But Paul, who manages the financial aspects of Andy's career, doesn't regret it at all today.

"I was all against being very open," Paul remembers, "doing interviews and telling the world we were gay. And I was so wrong. It was the smartest move to make I think."

"People always think that because you say you're gay, immediately your private life is exposed," Andy adds.

Open or not, Paul discovered almost immediately that no matter how much he and Andy loved one another, he would have to share Andy with other crucial relationships. First, there was Andy's openly straight songwriting partner, Vince Clark.

"That relationship is another love relationship that's not like ours," says Paul, who admits there were lots of jealousies in the beginning. "It's important that I don't become an obstacle in the way of that because I respect them and love them so much, as well."

It didn't help that in the early days Andy had a crush on Vince that lasted about a year.

"I was so shy in the beginning," Andy says, exhaling smoke into the air above his head. "And when we were in the studio for the first time I just used to sit and stare at him."

Then there were—and are—Andy's groupies.

"We were in Germany, and he had these six guys come up one right after the other," says Paul. "All tall, gorgeous looking, pushing me out of the way like I didn't exist. There's nothing you could do but sit back and go, 'Okay, I'll see you later.' "

Andy just shrugs and takes another drag of his cigarette.

Finally, there's always Andy's music.

"We went through the *Abbaesque* thing," Paul says, rolling his eyes, referring to Erasure's 1993 tribute to the Swedish band. "All we heard was ABBA."

"Over and over and over," Andy laughs.

"All night long. Now it's Blondie, because he's doing a cover of a Blondie song."

Andy says the songs he sings rarely have included references to his relationship with Paul. More than anything else he feels this is because their relationship has been so untroubled.

"When you're writing a love song there has to be turmoil," he says, "but I don't know enough about turmoil in relationships and stuff to really write this kind of song, so I just make it up."

A relationship free of turmoil seems uncommon when celebrities are involved. Paul thinks it's because celebrities tend to marry other celebrities—not the case here.

"Can you imagine Madonna and Sean Penn?" he asks. "I mean, great sex. But they're both actors. Those egos!"

Paul remembers always wanting to be involved with a musician some day—to feed Paul's love of music and the piano. Andy hoped to meet a farmer or at least somebody really down home.

"You've got to know how big your head is," Andy says, "how big you really are, and sort of keep it intact."

ANDREW MATTISON AND DAVID McWHIRTER

They wrote the book on love.

In 1983, psychologist Andrew Mattison and psychiatrist David McWhirter published the enormously successful *The Male Couple*, a study based on eleven years of research and interviews that explored how a huge sample of gay male couples lived and loved one another.

It was among the first books to analyze gay male behavior without applying a pathological model. In the 1970s, when Andrew and David began their research, most of the available literature equated homosexuality with mental illness. Their book was a truly pioneering work—which explains why it received the attention and awards it did, including two turns on *Oprah*, Australia's National Book Award, and a tribute at the International Congress of Sexology in India.

Andrew says the book "gave us the opportunity to look at what's there in the future [for us], as we interviewed couples that were together longer than we were at the time."

"It helped us as a couple in the sense that we were able to communicate at a much more intimate level pretty early on," David agrees. "We were able to talk to each other in ways that didn't push the other person away."

Not surprisingly, Andrew and David, whose relationship is now in its twenty-sixth year, consider male couples to be the most natural of human pairings. And they think straight couples can learn from the same-sex dynamic. "The general population see male couples modeling themselves after straight couples," says Andrew, forty-eight. "Well, the reality is that there's so much innovativeness and creativity within male couples that opposite sex couples have a lot to learn—*a lot to learn*. Heterosexuals have this gender expectation going into a relationship. 'You do this and I do that, because I'm the man and you're the wife.' And that isn't true with us. We have to negotiate."

One of the issues Andrew and David see as being less rigidly defined in gay relationships is the concept of fidelity. They don't

ANDREW MATTISON (RIGHT) AND DAVID McWHIRTER AT THE POOL OF THEIR ESCONDIDO HOME.

126

believe the right to marry is necessarily a priority for gays; like many of the couples they interviewed, they haven't been monogamous with each other throughout their relationship.

"It seems bizarre to me that as a [then] thirty-eight-year-old man coming out I was going to have exclusive sex with this other guy my whole life when the whole world was my oyster," David says.

Andrew points out that in his and David's relationship, as well as in those in their book, the men did not equate sexual exclusivity with fidelity: "That's a big leap. They were faithful to each other but didn't measure that sexually."

Of course, the research for *The Male Couple* was conducted before AIDS began to decimate the nation's gay male population, so the impact of the disease on relationships—and on fidelity—went unreported. But, says David, "AIDS is going to get cured . . . the closet problem continues."

"One of the things that distinguishes ourselves from some but not all the couples is that we're very, very out," Andrew adds. "And we find that outness a tremendous asset."

It wasn't always that way. When they met in the late 1960s at California's very conservative Jesuits University at Fairfield, both men were still in the closet. David, then on the faculty at the University of Southern California's medical school, worked at Fairfield with priests and nuns who were trying to exit the church because they wanted to marry or because they were gay. He met Andrew, a devout Catholic, when Andrew came to the Fairfield campus to take some summer courses.

"I had some inklings that I was gay," Andrew says, "but I went to mass and communion every day."

David, who also had been raised Catholic and had spent four years studying to become a Jesuit priest, kept his feelings buried much deeper. He was married (to a woman) and had two children.

"I really thought that if I got married it would all go away," he says, explaining. "I didn't know much about homosexuality or heterosexuality. I always had some attraction to men but I wasn't unattracted to women."

Over the next three years Andrew and David became very close. Andrew traveled to Europe with David's entire family. The two men remember understanding only that they had "an affinity" for each other and that what was developing between them was some sort of permanent relationship.

When they returned to California, David took a job at the State University of New York at Stoneybrook and relocated with his family to the East Coast. After a stint in VISTA, Andrew followed to get his graduate degree at the same university.

In the winter of 1971, David left his wife and moved in with Andrew. "I was thirty-eight and I couldn't go on living this burden." David recalls. His family's reaction was mixed. His wife took the news horribly, but his twelve-year-old daughter and fourteen-year-old son chose to live with their father.

"It was very natural," Andrew says. "We had a lot of years before we established ourselves as a couple. We knew somewhere in there where we were going. We took it a day, a week, a month at a time. But I didn't think it was going to be twenty-six years."

"We're incredibly happy," David says. "I mean, we continue to enjoy being together. We have two kids . . ."

"Two grandkids," Andrew adds.

The most difficult thing on the horizon may be David's impending retirement. He's almost sixty-five and wants to stop working as a professor and psychiatrist to gay men. Andrew, who works for a San Diego health group, is already having a hard time adjusting. Bottom line, he says, "I don't want to be in a different place than David is."